Secret Bi-Polar

Secret Bi-Polar

FINDING OUT AT SIXTY TWO

Jane Miller

To order additional copies of this book, contact:
Xlibris
1-888-795-4274
www.Xlibris.com
Orders@Xlibris.com
720391

Dedicated to the memory of Johnny

{1}

It was a hot summer day, in the middle of the summer, July eighteenth, nineteen fifty two and I was born, at five thirty eight in the morning. It was nothing elaborate, and no problems, just a plain old birth. I lived in a trailer on my father's parents land until I was two. I have many pictures of me while living at my grandparents when I was under two, crying a lot. Something was wrong with me but we didn't know it. When I was two we moved to our own house. We had two giant, over 30 feet tall, Holly trees (state tree) on each side of our front door. They started out as babies and over the years grew that tall. My parents always told me that when they bought the house they went out into a field and dug up the trees for me. Later in life this made my youngest brother so jealous of me. I was a daddy's girl. My father took me everywhere with him. He would go to a bar at the end of the street where he grew up and leave me in the truck. He would come out every so often to check on me and bring me potato chips or cheese crackers. I think it was for my mother's benefit that he took me. She probably figured he couldn't do anything with a child along. When he had a few beers in him he would put his country music on the record player and I would stand on his feet and we would dance around to Johnny Cash, Hank Williams, and others. We played checkers together a lot. When he would lay on the sofa to watch television I would lay there right next to him. I was only three or four. I sure loved my dad. I usually always sided with him when he and my mom got into arguments and fights, until when I was older I saw the truth. He started it and when the police came he lied through his teeth to them and had this horrible grin on his face while lying. When I was three or four years old I had to go to bed while it was still light outside; it must have been summer time. I remember crying and being very depressed. I could hear the little boy next door crying in his room also and a lot of times we would talk to each other through the screens. His father beat him a lot. He died last year and he was only a year older than me. It was very depressing. I felt his pain when we were children.

I would go into the bathroom medicine cabinet, take the jar of Vaseline jelly and the bottle of aspirin, eat all of it, then lay down to go to sleep while praying to GOD to please not let me wake up the next day. I always woke up. Then sadness consumed me again. Things weren't always bad, sometimes I was happy but it seems the sadness outweighed the happiness. There was a black cloud over my head and I always felt afraid like something bad was going to happen. I had a swing set and a swimming pool in the backyard. I was in the pool and on the swings all day until it was time to go to bed. When I was around eight a new neighbor moved into the house behind us. They had a son my age that was a little slow, a twelve year old daughter and a sixteen year old daughter. The boy was in my pool every day with me. We were best friends. One day his parents took me to his grandparent's farm in Pennsylvania. That was fun. We climbed in the barn in the hay and had a good time. I don't remember when but it wasn't long after they moved in. The two sisters were on their way home with the older sister driving and they got into an accident. The twelve year old was decapitated. She had the same name as me. My friend was never the same after that. I would run with the other neighborhood children playing hide and seek, Mother May I, tag and other games. Once a boy that was playing pushed me into the neighbor's hedge and she came out and yelled at me. I never cared for her after that. We would go to the baseball diamond to watch the little league play games. When it snowed I would pull my brother, Johnny, on the sled up and down the hill. Actually you could sled down our hill. We grew up on Buck Lane near the bottom of a pretty long hill. You could start your bike at the top of the street and just coast to half way around the next block. When I was six my dad bought my bike for me and the first thing I did was fall on a stone and the scar is still in the middle of my knee. I rode that bike all over the neighborhood, even down into the ranch house section. We lived in the brick two stories. Back then people didn't worry about child snatchings or molesters. They probably did worry but we were still allowed more freedom than today's world. I was six years old and allowed to walk the five blocks to elementary school. I was also allowed to walk to the small shopping center to buy penny candy, alone.

I used to like catching bumble bees in jars and caterpillars and Japanese beetles. I would pick the beetles off of the roses around the neighbors that had rose bushes. For some reason beetles love the flower part of a rose bush. I would also catch lightening bugs at night. My dad would pull the light off of them and stick it on my finger for a glow in the dark ring. One day I had some caterpillars and I had set them under a small bush that we had near the front of the house. They got out of their container and before I knew it the bush was full of caterpillars. My mom set the bush on fire and burned them up. Years later she died in a house fire right there.

One day my dad brought home a dog. It was for his hunting; a Chesapeake Retriever. My dad hunted everything. We had duck, goose, deer, muskrat, snapper turtle and GOD knows what else to eat because of my dad's hunting. The dog was supposed to retrieve the ducks out of the water after my dad shot them. One day he let me and my sister and brother take the dog for a walk. That dog ended up dragging us all over the neighborhood. He was too big for the three of us to control and we had to wait until the dog decided to go home before we got to go home. I never walked that dog again or any other big dog that I could not control. That is why Cleopatra is sitting here next to me waiting for the day that Anthony comes home. She will pull me until she starts to get tired of walking and then she will walk next to me, but it's only because she's tired.

My dad eventually got rid of that full grown dog and got one that was a puppy so he could raise it himself. Wouldn't you know it; he picked the runt of the litter and the poor dog got no bigger than a cocker spaniel. He gave her to me. I was about fourteen and I named her Holly. My friend that lived at the corner had a big black dog named Tiger that used to run all over the neighborhood. Since poor Holly wasn't allowed in the house, one day she turned up pregnant. She had her litter of pups. I found good homes for all of them and then one day I came home from school and she was gone. My dad said she ran away but I know he gave her to his cousin. He was always doing things like that, but I knew better. When I was younger I had a cat and of course she wasn't allowed inside. One snowy winter night she didn't come to the door to be fed. She never came back and my dad came home from work one night and said he saw a dead cat in the street two blocks away. I don't know if it was her, but I really think he gave her to his cousin. Those two were thick as thieves. His cousin had a daughter that his mother raised that was a year younger than me. I don't know why but she was not allowed to hang around with me and I was not allowed to hang around with her. Of course we were always together and during my running away from home period I would always go to her development and hide from my dad. I was such a brat. I think if I was on the medication that I am now on I would have been a much enjoyable kid to have around.

When I was nine my boyfriend was on the baseball team and his parents picked me up at my home and took me to an "away" game with them. I was happy then for a while. My one brother seemed to be like me. My other two sisters and brother seemed to be happy. But my brother Johnny and I were always depressed. My parents never took me anywhere to find out why I was so depressed and did the things I did. Maybe it was taboo back then. Also when I was nine I experienced my first death. I was extremely close to my grandfather. This was my father's father. I loved going to my father's parents'. My sister and I would spend the night there and our grandmother would sew a lot. She was always making us Barbie gowns and dresses for my sister and me. I didn't like the dresses for me because they were see through material. You had to wear an under shirt with it. You could see the under shirt completely. It was embarrassing. My grandmother always had a yard full of flowers and grape vines. I think I inherited my love for gardening from her. She would make homemade grape jelly and she was always buying my sister and I Sarah Coventry jewelry. She had an antique nightstand that we would sit at and put perfumes on. When you looked out her bedroom window there was a pony at the house next door. I always wished I could ride it but I never did. My grandmother cleaned offices down the street from her house and when I was small she would take me with her. I would sit at the desk and pretend I was working. When I grew up I always worked in an office except for once when I worked at Amazon for four months. She also did ironing for the Italians that lived in the big house at the end of the street. My father did not like Italians very much because he thought they were demeaning to his mother. I bet he was really mad when my last husband turned out to be an Italian.

When I was a teen I was a Girl Scout with my friend, Rita. We went to meetings every week, had parties on holidays and worked on badges. I had every badge that you could get. We went camping for two weeks one summer at a Girl Scout Camp in Maryland. We slept in tent cabins in sleeping bags. A prank of the girls was to spread toothpaste into someone's sleeping bag. I did not think it was very funny. Before I was a Girl Scout I was a "Brownie". That's what the younger girls were called. I spent many years as a Girl Scout.

When I was sixteen I wanted to go live with my father's mother, but she was sick with colon cancer. She died when I was almost seventeen and I was given the antique night stand. When I was going back and forth to Florida from the trailer on the bay I gave the night stand to my sister, who had always wanted it, because I didn't want to lose it. There is an empty lot where my grandparent's home used to be. It's like they were never there, but my memories of being there will live on as long as I do.

My mother's parents lived in a row house on the street in olde New Castle. My mother had eleven brothers and sisters, where my father had a sister and a brother who died in a house fire. When we went to their house I would sit on the front porch with my bedridden great grandfather and look out at the river. Their house had an outhouse and an indoor bathroom. They had a very large yard because they owned two row houses connected to each other. There was a tire hanging in a big tree in the back yard that my cousins and I would swing on. We would go ice skating on the dyke next to their house when we were sure it was really frozen good. I liked going to my grandparents'. It was a time when my parents just let me go and play with everyone else. These grandparents also had a grapevine. I remember my grandfather cutting the heads off of chickens and snapping turtles. There were peony flowers in the yard. I planted some in my yard last year. Peonies smell very good and they are nostalgic for me. My grandfather would do work at home for the Company and when I got older I did his billing for him to give to the Company. They used to be a chemical refinery in Delaware City. I would drive him down to the plant to deliver his work. One of my aunts lived in Philadelphia in the Italian section. My mother and father would take me and we would go up there to visit her and her Italian boyfriend who had two friends that were very muscular. My aunt had two cocker spaniel dogs. She died a mysterious death when I was fourteen. I remember the funeral and the Italian boyfriend coming and his two muscular friends came with him. My bedridden great grandfather lived next door to my grandfather and grandmother. One winter day my aunt told my cousin to watch the wood burning stove so that it didn't go out and leave our great grandfather in the cold. My cousin filled the stove to over flowing and set the house on fire. If it hadn't been for another aunt dragging my great grandfather out he would have died in the fire. The house was gone, so my family tore the other row house down and everyone pitched in and built a brick ranch house for my great grandfather and grandparents. After my great grandfather and grandmother passed, my grandfather moved to Smyrna, Tennessee to live with my aunt, who was also my Godmother. He stayed there until he passed. My youngest Uncle got the property and sold it for a lot of money and new condominiums that cost four hundred thousand dollars each were built there. The area is named after my uncle. My mother's maiden name was Miller.

In the early sixties we had a monster snow storm on March third. It may have been nineteen sixty two. The snow storm washed away all of the cottages where we stayed, all of the sand dunes at the ocean and did a lot of damage to people's homes. My fifty seven year old grandfather was shoveling snow that day and eleven o'clock that night my grandmother called and told my father that his dad had a heart attack and died. It was the first time I ever saw my dad cry. At the viewing my father took me up to the casket to tell my "poppie" good bye. He was just lying there looking straight ahead. My dad took his hand and ran it down my grandfather's face and closed his eyelids. Back then I guess the mortician's didn't close eyes. Poppie was my favorite. It seems GOD always took my favorite throughout my life. Maybe he thinks, or I'm not putting GOD first, but I wish things would change. I think I put GOD first, but maybe he doesn't. I learned at nine that I did not like funerals. In the third grade, I was still nine, there was a children's daily show called "Pixanne" that I used to watch on television. It was about a pixie that flew through the air and played a rock that was a piano. Children were sitting on the floor around the piano. I wrote to Pixanne and she sent me tickets to come on the show. My mother took me. We went to Wilmington, which is only four miles from our home, and got on a train and rode it to Philadelphia where the show was filmed. We walked to the studio and were directed to the show's set. I was sitting around the musical rock with the other children and Pixanne asked me if I could whistle. I was so scared that I said "No". I learned that there was a piano in the back of the rock and was rather disappointed. It was an experience I remember that was good.

We were dropped off at church every Sunday. I sang in the church choir and had confirmation and Holy Communion. We were not Catholic, Episcopalian, which is closest to Catholic. Yet I still tried to end my life several times. I was just not happy and that little black cloud and shoe followed me everywhere that I went. I almost drowned at a church picnic when I was nine. It's funny how your parents can drop you off at church on Sundays but then show up at the picnics. I don't get it. A group of people was playing in the water and I was following along with them. Before I knew it I was over my head and I had to keep jumping up to get air, then I would go back under and I did this a few times. Had my mother not been sitting on the blanket on land watching me I wouldn't be here. She ran and jumped into that water and swam out to me and saved my life. She laid me on the blanket and all these church people came around, the pastor, also. I was embarrassed. I closed my eyes and pretended to sleep. Well all that jumping was tiring.

Every summer my dad would take us tenting for two weeks at the Indian River Inlet. This was a big tenting ground and trailer park. I can remember lying on the giant sand dunes and rolling down them with my brothers and sisters while my dad surf fished. We were allowed to run off but had to stay close by. My father always had a boat and we were always on the Delaware River crabbing or just boating. We would go crabbing many other places also, wherever the crabs seemed to be. I can remember bringing home a bushel of crabs that we caught and cooking them and eating them on the patio while drinking beer and sodas. Crabbing was fun. I liked it a lot. You tied a raw chicken neck to the end of a piece of string and hung it over the side of the boat. After a while, while holding a net in one hand, you slowly, slowly pulled the rope up to the surface of the water. As you got near the surface you could see if a crab was hanging onto that chicken neck and if he was you swooped under him with your net and into the bushel basket he went. We had many good times from childhood into adult married life crabbing and eating them on the patio. It was a way of life. They were good times for my sisters and brothers and me. Until I was a young teenager I never saw a beer in my mother's hands. She always drank Pepsi. My dad did the drinking, every day and night. My dad stormed the beaches at Normandy and Okinawa. He also was in World War II in the United States Navy. After all that I guess he was entitled to his beer. At least it wasn't drugs or hard liquor. There would be another drunken fight and I would end up a nervous wreck again. We also went to Ocean City, Maryland during these summer vacations. One time I fell asleep on the beach and when I woke up I looked like a lobster. That night my family was going to the boardwalk to ride the rides and have fun. I lay in the back seat of the car, throwing up and in very much pain the entire time they were having their fun. I think my mother should have known better than to let me sleep in the sun. She had to know I was going to get burned. In my later years I had skin cancer cut out of my back. My two sisters did, too. Soon the tenting ground closed in the early nineteen sixties and my father started renting a cottage for us to go to every year. We went there every summer for a two week vacation. I had a girlfriend who had her own boat, a small rowboat with a small motor, and she would take me with her. We would ride the boat all around the bay. You could walk out to the middle of the bay and the water was only knee deep. My father always had a boat and at the time of the cottage, he would take me water skiing. It seemed if I wasn't doing something, that I was sad and very depressed. Keeping active seemed to help a lot. My mind needed to be busy so the depression didn't take over. My father was a functioning alcoholic. Almost every night there was terrible fighting and screaming in the house, many times being broken up by the police. Needless to say, I had irritable bowel syndrome and didn't find out until I was in first grade at the age of six; and missing a lot of school. A lot of times if we were going to the beach or an amusement park, I would get so excited that I would get stomach aches and diarrhea. Directly across the Delaware River, from us, there was an amusement park. My mother would take us there a lot while my father was at work. They had the biggest swimming pool I have ever seen in my life. I still have not seen a bigger one. Every time my mother announced that we were going to Riverview I would get so excited that I would get diarrhea. I was usually okay after we got there and started riding rides and swimming.

I lived close enough to the school that I could walk there and home but I was afraid to leave the house and my stomach would start churning and rolling around and I got a stomach ache just thinking about having to go out. . Also, my chest would get pains and I would get anxious and nervous and not want to leave the house. My parents were always calling the doctor to find out what was wrong with my stomach. No one ever knew what was wrong with my stomach and they never tried to find out what was wrong with my mind. My first grade teacher lived two houses from me. Around Easter time I missed over thirty days of school. The teacher and all the class mates made me an Easter basket and the teacher dropped it off home to me one evening. Every day I went to school I was a nervous wreck and scared to death, I barely spoke to anyone. When I was in third grade I had to have my tonsils and adenoids taken out. I got to stay out of school a few days again and this made me very happy. For some reason I did not want to leave the house. I was happiest just staying home. With all the drunken fighting I was diagnosed with generalized anxiety disorder. This was my life and when I was twelve, I remember trying to over dose on some Darvocet that my mother had. My parents found me on the bathroom floor and took me to the hospital. They made me throw up and I had to stay overnight for observation. At this time my mother let me go live with my aunt. I stayed at my aunt's house with my cousins for a few days, happily, and then went back home. The depression came back again. It feels like a dark cloud is hanging over your head and you are waiting for the other shoe to drop. It's a horrible feeling. My two sisters and my remaining brother have the same diseases that I have. They too never found out until they were in their 40s and 50s that they have bipolar disorder and manic depressive disorder. When I was in the sixth grade I was a school safety patrol guard. Funny, considering my opinion of authority figures.

{2}

Life continued this way, and I had problems with authority figures and going to school. I would cut classes every day. A boy that lived in our neighborhood would pick me up so that I didn't have to make the long walk to school every day. He also liked me and asked me to go to the Homecoming dance with him. I accepted and could not wait for October twenty fourth to come. On Friday night, October twenty third, nineteen sixty eight, the boy, Jason, called me and said that one of our classmates had his parent's Bonneville convertible for the night. He said a bunch of our friends were going riding around and did I want to come too. I told him "No" because my father would never allow me to go riding around with a carload of boys. The next morning when I got up my mother told me that Jason and another one of my friends was killed the night before. They were going too fast around a curve and sideswiped a bunch of trees. Two boys were thrown from the car. Jason had a viewing but the other boy was too badly hurt for anyone to see so they kept his coffin closed. I've kept the newspaper clippings all these years and think to myself that I could have been in that car and possibly gotten killed at the ripe young age of sixteen.

One day I cut school with another boy that liked me and my dad's cousin's girl and some other classmates. The boy had a falcon car and we rode around all day. We rode up north toward Pennsylvania going up and down all the one way back roads and hills. The scenery was beautiful and I always wished I could live like that one day. We were riding along and I guess we were going too fast because the boy overturned the car into a ditch. Everyone got out of the car and up righted it and we continued on our journey.

On my sixteenth birthday my best friend and I were riding around with our boyfriends and they stopped and bought a small bottle of whiskey and a six pack of beer. We went to the Park in historic New Castle and parked. I took one drink of the whiskey, which is the nastiest stuff that I ever tasted, and the police pulled up. Needless to say all four of us were arrested. They took us to the police station and because we were under age they called our parents. My mother grew up in New Castle and she knew everyone and her brother, my uncle, used to be a policeman. She came after me and she had been drinking so she told the police, "Today's her birthday she can have a drink for her birthday". They all joked for a while and talked and then we left. My girlfriend's mother came in there and smacked her around. After she saw how my mother was treating me she stopped and she and my mother started talking. My friend spent the night at my house that night in the tent in our back yard and we ended up sneaking out of the tent and meeting back up with the boys. When we went to court for the drinking under age charge I got a twenty five dollar fine. Things have really changed since I was sixteen.

I never really had a boyfriend until I met John. We had our own group in the neighborhood and if you were male and my friend then you were my boyfriend. I had a lot of those, but the only one I ever dated or messed around with was John. I knew him and loved him since I was seventeen and he was sixteen.

One summer my mom and my girlfriend's mother got tickets to take a trip on a bus to the Atlantic City casinos. I think they were given spending money and vouchers, too. While they were in the casino my friend and I wandered the boardwalk. We had pictures taken of us holding a big bottle of whiskey and in jail. The Road Runner car was popular at that time and we had two friends that owned one. My girlfriend and I got tee shirts at Atlantic City that had the road runner on them and the saying "Beep Beep Yuras". I have it on in my jail picture which is in my albums outlining my entire life. We had a really good time at Atlantic City and coming home on the bus was fun, too.

Everyone at school said I should be a model. When our senior pictures were taken the photographer put mine on display. I told my parents that I wanted to be a model. My father said I'd never be a model or amount to much. That was a horrible thing to say to me. One of my friends heard him say it also. He wanted me to join the Navy because he was in the Navy. I wanted to be a housewife if I couldn't be a model. I think he held me back at home. Actually I KNOW he was holding me back. It was probably the money. He probably thought he would have to pay too much for me to be a model. Heaven forbid that he shouldn't have any beer money because his daughter wanted to be a model and it cost too much. A friend of mine since tenth grade (nineteen sixty eight) still tells me today that it was a shame my father did that to me because everyone thought I would make a good model. I was tall and skinny and I always had the most stylish clothes. After all, I was working and after giving my mom fifty dollars I bought all the best clothes and jewelry that my money could afford.

When I started high school in nineteen sixty eight they had just started segregation. All of these African Americans were bussed out from Wilmington to our school and they took some of our kids and bussed them into the Wilmington schools. None of the parents or kids liked the bussing idea. We were always having riots at my high school between the blacks and the whites. Somebody was always picking a fight and everyone would gang up on who was fighting and we would get mad and leave the school without permission and ride around it in our vehicles beeping the horns. We were on the five o'clock news quite a few times. It was bad in nineteen sixty nine. The blacks came to our neighborhood and threw bottles and bricks at people and cars. One of our friends threw something back and he ended up getting arrested. We didn't think that was fair so a big gang of us went to court eleven, where they took our friend, and sat out front protesting. We made the front page of the newspaper again. This time our pictures were in the paper. No matter how bad no one liked segregation, it was here to stay.

One day when I went home from school, my mother was very mad. She was holding a letter from the school that told her I was always cutting class. She took me to the school and pulled me by my hair into the principal's office. After this I was supposed to go to school, however I continued to cut class. I was in my senior year and graduation was coming up in June. I was failing Civics which was needed to graduate. A friend of mine found out that the teacher was having a birthday and that this was the last year he would teach at our school. My friend and I bought him a giant birthday cake. We had the baker put "goodbye and good luck" on the cake. He passed us and we graduated. For our Senior trip the class went to New York City. We saw a play on Broadway, the Rockettes, went shopping and had dinner and finally climbed to the head of the statue of liberty. All of the pictures that I took chronicle my life. If it had not been for my mother dragging me into the school and taking me to school and driving me there to watch me to go into the school; I would not have graduated. Many times she would drop me off and watch me go in the doors and I would walk right out the back doors. I was horrible. I managed to go to the senior prom, however, but by this time I was drinking beer along with everyone else. My date and I and the group we were with left the prom early and went to a party and got drunk. I managed to get my prom picture taken before we left. Now I wish I would have just stayed at the prom. That's one not so good memory that should be a good one. I didn't know it then but I know it now, my mom was my best friend. I graduated high school and got a job at a whole sale cigarette company. I was making a little over a dollar an hour running vending machine money through a money counter and counting the paper money by hand. I was in accounts receivable. I liked the job. Every day at four o'clock I would call my mom so that I could listen to" Dark Shadows" in the background. What a job. Every Friday when I got paid the first thing I did was give my mom fifty dollars. I then spent the rest of my pay on clothes and jewelry. Also on Friday nights after work, two people that I worked with and I would go out drinking and partying. Yes, drinking. If you come from an alcoholic family eventually you start drinking, too. However I did quit when I was thirty and still very rarely drink alcohol. We would have the best of fun. Just the three of us; one boy, who liked me, and a gay girl, who also liked me. There was no fooling around or anything, just hanging out and enjoying each other's company. Many a day the girl would pick me up to go to work and I would still be drunk or high from the night before. I saw her not to long ago. She lives in her parents' house on the street one over from where I grew up. Anyway, they both knew I was crazy about John.

My first credit account, at age 17 was at a jewelry store. I put a mother's ring on lay a way. It was really nice. When my mom died I told my sister to put the ring in the casket with her. But, knowing my sister, the ring is at her house and she has it. I wasn't allowed to see my mother when she died.

I was more interested in a boy from my neighborhood then I was in working and that would be John. My dad had gotten me a little blue '68 chevy corvair, stick shift, so that I could drive myself back and forth to work. I used to give another girl that worked there a ride, also. I had the car one month and totaled it. It was raining out and I turned to the girl in the passenger seat and when I turned back the traffic had stopped and I slammed on the brakes but I rear ended the car in front of me. We had to go to the hospital. I had a broken nose and one of her teeth got knocked out. My insurance covered her tooth and got her a new one, but I never got another car. I guess my parents thought I was going to end up killing myself. That one would be accidental. Actually I hadn't had a bout with depression for quite some time now. I was too busy concentrating on working, John and partying. It's when my mind was not doing anything that the depressed thoughts would come.

{3}

At eighteen I left home and all the battles and moved in with my boyfriend and his family. At least there were no drunken fights there and I was not a nervous wreck. My boyfriend was in the way of his father's second marriage and his step mother put him away in a boy's home in January. I was so mad that I went to their house one night and poured split pea soup and sugar in her Cadillac gas tank. The witch. I never knew the outcome of that little stunt because after John turned eighteen and got out of the group home we didn't associate with his father anymore. In fact I don't even think we invited him to the wedding, just John's mother. I hitchhiked to where they were keeping John, to visit him. Sometimes his social worker gave me a ride and his social worker was very nice and trying to help us and I went back home not knowing I had gotten pregnant New Year's Eve. Living at home was tolerable because I knew I was having a baby and I was thrilled because I now have someone to love and for them to love me. I kept telling my mother and father that I wanted to get married to him. They said I was too young and could not understand why I was adamant about getting married. We were talking and having a civil conversation and finally it was like a light bulb went off in my father's head and he said "Unless, you are pregnant" and he asked me if I was pregnant. I said "yes" and I was beaming from head to toe. "Well that explains everything." He said. He said I did not have to get married. That I could live at home and have the baby. All I could think of is when they got into those fights; I didn't want the baby to be subjected to that. I was head over heels in love or lust with the baby's father, anyway. In March my baby's father turned eighteen and he left the boy's home and moved in with his aunt and uncle. Everyone knew I was pregnant and I was there every night. One night my boyfriend said, "Well I guess we have to get married". I told him my dad said I didn't have to get married. But we were going to get married. My sister was my maid of honor and we got gowns and had some excitement in that house for once. We got married in the Church on the Green, where my mom and dad got married and I got baptized. Quite a bit of people turned out even though you could tell I had a baby bump. I was five months. After the ceremony we climbed into the back seat of a friend's car and rode all through the neighborhood beeping the horn. We then headed back to my house for a small reception. We cut the cake together and then I changed and we left and went to a motel. People who have more money go on cruises and vacations. I was happy because I was with my first and only true love. We went to live with his aunt and uncle for a while and then finally got a small one bedroom apartment in the city. It was the second floor of some old couple's house. They didn't seem too happy when they saw I was pregnant. My uncle and dad had to use a ladder to lift all the furniture into a second floor bedroom window. I don't know how they did it.

In July the social worker helped my husband get hired. He worked the night shift from the time he was eighteen until he died at forty three. I guess we were at the apartment about a month and my son was born. His father had just brought us home from the hospital and a friend of his knocked on the door and wanted him to go downtown with him. I protested to no avail. He never came back. They got arrested for having a needle and syringe and a bag of heroine. I never knew he was doing this! My mom sent my sister over to bring me and the baby home. During the time that my husband was in jail his old social worker came around and took me to his work to pick up his check so I could pay bail. This surely was the beginning of the end, but I was so in love with him. We were separated with my husband in jail.

My son, Joey and I moved back to my mom's. My dad's words rang in my ears. "You're too young to get married, what do you want to get married for?" We were only there for a few days and John was set free. Back to the little apartment we went. Everything turned out okay. I think he got probation or something trivial, but now I was stuck with him doing drugs. He said he would stop. Things were starting to get cramped in the little apartment so we rented a two bedroom at Forest Hills. We had so many arguments over little things. We got along good then all of a sudden we were arguing and I'm quite sure a lot of it was my fault. Why was I doing these things? I loved my husband to death and I was picking arguments with him. What is wrong with me? Who do I think I am? When things got too crowded at Forest Hills we moved into a two bedroom at a complex with an in ground pool. We started arguing a lot. He was never there. I was always mad and argumentative. Did I inherit this? A girl I used to hang around with was the lifeguard. We were happy there. When Joey was a year and a half I asked John if we could have another baby and he said, "No". Now I know that he was right. We went to concerts and saw Rod Stewart, Grand Funk Railroad, Billy Preston and many others. We went to clubs and people made circles around us to watch us dance. Especially at the old Philadelphia Spectrum, which is now gone. This was also the time that a porno film was popular called "Deep Throat". My husband and our best friends wanted to see it but you had to be eighteen. The girl in our group was still seventeen. I did not want to watch a porno movie and especially one with such a title as it had. Without anyone knowing, I telephoned the theater and told the clerk that we would be coming to see the movie but one of our people was not eighteen. I said that the clerk would recognize us because I would have wet hair. I took a shower to get ready to go to the movie and made sure I washed my hair. When we got to the theater to buy the tickets the clerk looked at me and then carded all of us. Naturally my girlfriend's showed that she was seventeen and we were turned away. No one ever found out that I did that.

My dad never really liked John because he had long hair. I guess he didn't know that his daughter was also into the Hippie scene, too. His not caring for John didn't bother me because in all actuality my dad did not like any boy that showed an interest in me. He got over it and I think when Joey was seventeen John and my dad met up at my current husband and my house and they were civil to each other. Also, John outgrew the long hair and was balding.

Why did I ever think that moving from apartment to apartment would help us? I would pack his lunch and send him off to work the night shift every day. I stayed at home with Joey who was one and a half now. One night everything shattered. I was talking to John's sister on the phone and she told me that the company was retooling which meant that the entire plant was shut down for two or three weeks. My beloved was pretending to go to work and only GOD knows where he really was until midnight every night. One night I took Joey to my sister-in-law so she could watch him while I went looking for him. Talk about possessive and vengeful, that's me! I got a friend, James, to drive me around and wouldn't you know it, we came right up on Charlie's car with my husband in the back seat with a girl. Charlie saw us and tried to lose us but he couldn't. He went around a corner that was a ramp to get on another road and he flipped over onto the hill. All of them got out of the car and ran up and over the hill. Charlie was an old friend since I was twelve years old. I went home to our apartment. Well, my dad was right; we were too young to get married. He had only been eighteen for two months and I was turning nineteen in two months. Now the girlfriends and boyfriends started. It was horrible. I hated it. I loved him. I didn't want other people involved. One night he was having a little party with his friends and we were arguing. I got a razor blade from the medicine cabinet and held it over my wrist. I looked at him and he looked at me and said, "I dare you". In one swift motion I just about took my hand off. He ran to call an ambulance and try to stop the bleeding. The ambulance came and took me to the hospital. I remember waking up, on the way to surgery, and seeing my mom standing there holding Joey. I stayed in the hospital for about three days then went home to my mother's. The men from the ambulance came to the house to see me. They told me they almost lost me for a minute. That was nice of them. John was busy having parties at the apartment. I guess he didn't pay the rent because the next thing I know, there's a padlock on the door. One specific neighbor thought it her duty to let me know everything that went on in that apartment before it got padlocked. I got a boyfriend while living at my parent's but it didn't last. I really loved John. We might have fought a lot but he was all I wanted, except for my baby. He was really partying it up though with different girls and one of his girlfriends had the nerve to put their engagement in the newspaper while we were still married. I was furious!

Joey and I would go boating with my mom and dad a lot. They were always drinking beer. We would go to the Delaware River and put the boat into the water then go crabbing. Even though my parents' were drinking we still had a lot of fun except one time. They got into an argument and my mother started walking and we couldn't find her. Joey and I rode home with my dad to make sure he got there safely and put the boat in the driveway, then I got the car and went back to look for my mom. I found her in a restaurant at the end of a row of stores overlooking the river, eating king crab legs with some man. I joined them and when they were finished the man took us on a yacht that he had docked there. He was hired to deliver it to Florida. It had a big radar thing that moved around on top of the boat. You could live on it. There was a washer and dryer and everything you needed to live on it. My mother was considering going to Florida with the man to deliver the boat. I guess I ruined that for her because I kept reminding her of my father, her husband. We would sit at my mom and dad's patio and eat crabs, shrimp, beer and sodas every summer. All of my brothers and sisters were there except for the one who skipped state in the early seventies. One day I had lit the grill to warm it up to cook chicken on it and while it was warming I went to the bathroom. When I came downstairs I opened the lid and a gust of fire burst out at me and singed my eyebrows and hair. Propane still scares me to this day.

John and I went our separate ways and divorced five years later. Now that I look back I should have never divorced him, because twenty years later he was coming back to me. I just didn't know it at the time. Who does? He only came to see our son at Christmas and Easter. On these days he would take our son to visit his grandparents. I never had our son during Easter or Christmas until later in the evening.

{4}

While living with my parents I got a job at the neighborhood. A woman hired me, but when I started working a man was my manager. He was very good looking and it wasn't long before we were dating and I was filing for divorce and we were married. Now that I look back I probably should have stayed with him. Every time my first husband came around, my hopes would get high and I would hope we would get back together and I would divorce my present husband. My son's father was the love of my life. He never came back. He said after being married to me that he would never get married again. He said he would be a "lifelong bachelor" and the love of my life stayed a bachelor, dating lots of women but never going to get married again. I lived with my second husband and his family and my best friend married his brother. We had many good times together but I just couldn't get John out of my mind. Everyone got divorced. My best friend had two children with her husband and when the son was twenty six, about four or five years ago, he hung himself in their basement. I heard he was on heroine. He left a girl that was pregnant and when the baby was born my friend told me, "At least we have the baby". I thought to myself, "I'd rather have my son". I went to the florist and picked a nice house plant with other flowers in it and had it delivered to her. I wrote on the card, "My heart is breaking for you", and it was.

I had another friend who lived down the street from where I grew up. He and I were best friends our whole life. My mom would walk down the street to visit his mom once in a while. He was a volunteer fireman and when we were eighteen he fell off the back step of the fire truck and got hurt very badly. He was in the hospital a long time. My mom and I went to the hospital to see him. Years later when I was living in Florida he overdosed on heroin and died.

Life went on and my mother helped me get on welfare and helped me get an apartment in the old army barracks. My son and I lived there from the time he was three until nine. He was always outside playing with his friends. I was at the apartment by myself and I was very lonely and the depression came back fast. We didn't have a car so now I was a welfare mom. A lot of times Joey and I would ride the bus into the city to meet my mom and we would have lunch and drinks then we would ride our respective buses back to our homes. Joey played the alto sax and was in a Christmas play when he was in elementary school. I went with my neighbors and Joey's dad went with his girlfriend. All of the children stood to sing Christmas carols and when they were finished they sat down. Joey was still standing all alone on the stage and the teacher had to go tell him to sit down. My son, the star! Joey's dad always came to get him on Christmas and Easter. He did not see him any other time of the year. I never had my son on those two holidays until late at night. Alex and I went to court for child support for Joey and the judge ordered someone who worked for Chrysler and made sixty thousand dollars a year to pay me ten dollars a week for child support. The judge was either nuts or the system was. I never figured it out.

People moved next door to me. It was a husband and wife, two small girls and the wife's brother. (Bo) I ended up marrying the wife's brother which was number three and on the rebound or possibly because of my crazy mental status. The next door neighbor was a long haul truck driver with an eighteen wheeler. Bo was his brother in law. One night my mom and dad had an argument and my mom came to stay with me for a while. She ended up staying a month while I rode in the truck to Detroit, Green Bay and other places. Needless to say the neighbor's marriage broke up and the ex-husband asked if I wanted to travel for a while since my mom was there. She encouraged me to go and I called her at almost every truck stop. I even got to drive the truck from Wilmington to Detroit. It was a very nice experience for a twenty something girl. Bo, my third husband, was always drinking beer. I hated living there in the ghetto with a drunk. Of all people, here I was with someone who had a can of beer attached to one of his upper extremities all the time. GOD help me and Joey!! Bo and I had a big argument at Christmas time once and he knocked the tree down then punched me in my face and broke my nose. Finally my mom and dad came and moved me and Joey back home. My dad took me to the hospital to get my nose reset. We didn't stay at my mom and dad's long because it just wasn't the same. I was so argumentive and hateful. I felt I didn't deserve all I was handed. I went and got an apartment not far from the house. I took the husband who broke my nose back and he moved into the apartment with us. The apartment was on the third floor and one night we had another fight and he hit me again. It just so happened at the same time someone was banging loudly on the apartment door. Bo thought it was the police but it was actually my sister! Before he knew who was at the door he jumped out the third story window and fell through the tree that was outside the window. He landed on the ground and took off running for who knows where because he didn't know that it was only my sister and her jokester boyfriend. He was gone for a while and then came back with a cast on his leg. We stayed together still. We only had been in the apartment a month and my section eight papers came through. I found a very nice apartment in a nice area and we moved into it on December sixteenth. I was very happy in that apartment. My son had a good friend and I got a job driving a school bus for the state. Joey and I came home one night to find my mother sitting on the steps in the hallway. She had an argument with my father and somehow made it to my apartment. She slept in Joey's bed and went back home when she felt like it. Another time I was at my apartment watching TV and I got a call from the police station. They had found my mother walking all alone on the country back roads. It must have been ten o'clock at night and dark! I rushed to the police station to get her. She and my dad had an argument on the way home from the boating area and she got out and started walking and he left her. She stayed at my apartment until she was ready to go home. Another time she called me on the phone crying and said that my dad cut her with a knife. I was so scared and upset I sped all the way to their house just to get there at the same time the police did. This was the time I saw my dad lie through his teeth and the evil in him. I told the police that I was going to bring my mom home with me. She stayed as long as she wanted. As much as they fought, they did love each other. I found that out when my mom passed in the house fire. My dad came over my house and he was crying and he told me that he loved her very much.

{5}

One day my sister called me up to know if I wanted to go to a bar with her. I had been in that apartment for so long and I was lonely and could feel the depression coming back. I had bought a cheap car and I picked her up and we went to the bar in the city that also has a restaurant. She called her friend and she was coming there to meet us. This is where I met my fourth and last husband. He was the one who did the most damage to me and the children; mentally and emotionally. I had gotten up to go use the bathroom and when I came back a gorgeous Italian man was sitting in my seat. I told him, "You are sitting in my seat". He moved over and I slid in. We started talking and I asked him his birthdate. I was on the prowl for a Scorpio; however he said his birthday was July seventeenth. I didn't believe him because my birthday was the eighteenth. I made him show me his I D. My sister and her friend took my car to go to a party and I went with Alex to go to his house. I was pretty drunk. I met his mother and she gave me some dancing shoes to wear because we told her we were going dancing. However, I ended up lying on his bed puking my insides out with a terrible headache. He got wet washcloths and put them on my forehead. And as sick as I was, he tried to jump my bones! I very politely told him "No thank you". After that night I made it a point to be in the club that he usually frequented. We would dance a lot and we were pretty good. People would stand around and watch us. He did not like me when I was drinking, though. He made that clear in no uncertain terms, however, he continued to drink his mixed drinks and I didn't know it, but his cocaine, also.

Joey was ten years old now. It took me ten years to finally get over his dad and marry someone for life. Alex was an ex-Marine. He did two tours in Viet Nam and was exposed to Agent Orange twice. Everything was good with him in the beginning. We played tennis, went to the Park, the zoo and just hung out all the time while Joey was in school. I was happy. Alex was an only child; Italian and let me tell you, he was soooooo good looking. He lived in a third floor apartment at his mother's house in the city. I didn't know it but his girlfriend, who was pregnant, lived there too. Alex and I were always together. He would ride me to work at the bus yard and in nineteen eighty two when my grandfather came to say goodbye to us because he was moving to Tennessee to live with my Godmother; Alex was there. Somewhere in between meeting him and my grandfather's visit Alex had moved into the apartment with Joey and me. After my grandfather's visit in March, he died that August. One night when Alex and I were in bed he began choking me. I don't know if I said something or what set him off. My sister later told me that he was doing a lot of cocaine every night with his uncle, who was Alex's age. This was a warning that I ignored. I was still driving the school bus when I found out I was three months pregnant. Alex never asked me to marry him. His way was to give me a sculptured cigarette lighter with my initials with his last name on the side. On January seventeenth, nineteen eighty three we were married in city hall. When I was three months pregnant Alex and I had an argument and he punched me in the stomach. He knew I was pregnant. I thought that this man is so cold. I made him get out of Joey and my apartment. It wasn't long before he was back. I drove the school bus until I was about five months pregnant. I never was one for working out of the home. I was so happy to be allowed to just be a housewife. Mentally and emotionally everything was great! When my maternity leave was up and it was time to go back to driving the bus, I was pregnant again! Little Anthony was three months old and I was pregnant. The six months that I drove the school bus counted when I retired with the state, years later, in getting my Blue Cross paid for by the state. I pay thirty seven dollars a month for Blue Cross and prescription coverage until I die. Once we had the second child, a daughter and we named her Sue, we started looking for a house. Alex was going to buy us a house! I was thrilled! I had never been so happy! I didn't know it but my sister had taken Alex aside and told him, "I'm glad she's with you. She's had a hard life". No one knew about the bad things. They thought well of him and liked him a lot. I guess it was me he didn't like. I know he didn't like me, let alone love me. I looked in the newspaper every day and I found a small ranch house not far from my parents' development and it had an in ground pool. We went to look at it and when the man opened the door all of us ran to the back windows to see the pool. We bought the house in June of nineteen eighty five. I was never so happy. I had what I thought was the best looking Italian husband, a home with an in ground pool and a thirty thousand dollar boat that could sleep six Best of all I had my three great children. I looked around at my husband and thought to myself that I had to be the luckiest girl in the world. We bought a purebred German shepherd puppy for the kids when the puppy was six weeks old. We named her Roxanne. As she grew older she became very protective of the house, her yard and her family, especially the children. Every holiday we had to spend all day at Alex's mother's house. We never got to my parent's until after dinner. I didn't think that was fair. He was being selfish.

It didn't last long. In the spring of 1986 Alex and I were installing a storm door on the back of the house. I could hear fire whistles blowing off in the distance. The phone rang around 8:30 and when I answered it my girlfriend, who lived on the street behind my mom, said my mother's house was on fire. I asked her if it was bad and she said she couldn't tell. She said a lot of black smoke was coming out of it. Alex and I let Joey, who was now 14, watched Sue and we took Anthony with us. The street going up to my childhood home was blocked off by fire trucks and police. A row of cars sat motionless on that street. I got out of our car and started running to my house, jumping over fire hoses along the way. I passed my dad sitting in his truck with the door opened and I yelled, "Where's mom?" He just shook his head. I continued on to the house. About a hundred people stood around a yellow crime scene tape. A bruiser of a female firefighter walked out the front door and went down the sidewalk. I yelled, "Where's my mom?" She just ignored me. I was devastated. I wanted to die. I stayed in a deep depression for three years then I remembered my mother had said she wished one of her girls was a nurse. She died in that fire and I knew she was depressed. Every day I went over there and she would cry because my dad and my sister met at the local club and drank until my mom was asleep. I blamed my dad and my sister for my mother's death for years. I went to see my dad a couple of years after her death, but then I didn't see him for at least fifteen or twenty years again.

When Anthony was about eleven he had a bad reaction to Ceclor. He swelled up like a balloon and all of his joints were in pain. He was crying from the pain and his throat was closing in and he was going into anaphylactic shock. Alex carried him to the car and we rushed him to the Children's Hospital. They said he had an allergic reaction to the Ceclor and they admitted him. They put a cot in his room and I stayed with him. He was in the hospital four days before he was released. One day I got a wheelchair and hooked his IV to it and wheeled him all over the hospital on a tour. In the basement there was a huge swimming pool that was no longer in use. We had a lot of fun, but I was glad when he was able to come home. Now he never takes Ceclor.

June nineteen eighty nine off to the community college I went for Registered Nursing. Not for me, for my mom. I also knew the marriage was going to end the same way they always end and I would need skills to get another job to support myself and three children. I sent the kids to school, took care of the housework, and studied. Alex acted like he was jealous of what I was doing. He always said I was competing with him. Of course there was no competition. He dropped out of school in the seventh grade and I have three years of college. When we got divorced he said that he thought that when I started college that I got a boyfriend. He had no idea how hard Registered Nursing was. I constantly had to study. I had to learn all about the human body right down to what our atoms are made up of. I was also taking care of three children and sending them to school and doing housework. I didn't have time for a boyfriend, nor did I want one. Alex never confronted me at the time. He made his home on the sofa and that's where he stayed until we divorced.

I never finished nursing. I dropped out on Valentine's Day nineteen ninety two. I just woke up one morning and said "this isn't for me". If my mom was alive she would have gotten me through it. She would have been my support system. Instead, I quit two weeks before graduation. Within a month I was hired by the hospital and went to work.

I did not go to work until Sue went to school. While Sue and Anthony were young I was always taking them to parks and the beach. We went to the Park a lot and the Zoo a lot. In the summer we would have pool parties. All the kids on our street were my children's best friends in the summer. Amazing! We went to Augustine Beach, a small beach on the Delaware River that my father used to take us to when we were kids. I took Anthony and Sue to Chuck E Cheese and Show Biz Pizza quite a bit. I was a little kid when I was with them. I was always looking for places to go and things for us to do while their father was at work and not at home. One day we went on a hunger and homeless walk through the city of Wilmington with my friend. We got all kinds of freebies and had fun doing the walk as well. I don't think we finished it though because it was so long. Someone picked us up in a car and drove us back to the starting point. It started at the Zoo. My kids loved to climb the rocks on the Brandywine River. There were huge rocks that you could jump across and the water was very shallow if there at all. I have our entire life in pictures in picture albums. When I have passed it is my hope that my children will look at the pictures and see that we had a lot of good times, not just bad times. Most of the time we were in our pool every summer from morning until night, only getting out to get something to eat.

One day I was driving Anthony to football practice. It was his tenth birthday. We were stopped at a red light and a tractor trailer came around the corner and the back wheels ran over the car behind us and shoved it into us. We didn't think we were hurt, but a month later I couldn't stand the neck and back pain any longer. I went out of work on FMLA. I was off of work from September until February. As I started to feel better I started to take the kids places. One day we went to Hershey Park. Sue was nine and Anthony was ten. We got on the roller coaster and no one saw that the bar was not laying across Sue's stomach. She was sitting in the cart with me and Anthony was in the cart in front of us. His bar was tight against his stomach. The first big hill we went down Jessica slid under the bar and onto the floor of the cart. There was an opening at the side where you get in and out. There was no door on it. I rode the entire ride with one leg twisted like a pretzel blocking the entrance to the ride so that she did not fall off, while holding her around her shoulders with my right arm. My left arm held onto Anthony sitting in front of us. I don't think I have ever ridden a roller coaster since then. My daughter could have been killed that day. After that we chose less dangerous rides. We rode a ride through the Hershey factory that showed how the chocolate was made and the candy was made. All in all we had a good day at Hershey Park.

Another day we went to Sesame Street. They were a little younger and their father came with us this time. I had to buy a bathing suit there because there were so many water rides that adults could ride with their children. I have lots of pictures of our day at Sesame Street with Cookie Monster hugging Anthony and Big Bird hugging Sue. Early in the marriage, when the children were very young, Alex and I got along pretty good. It was as the children grew that we grew apart.

One day Alex took Joey and Anthony out on the boat. There was a tornado warning and I was constantly watching for them to come home. They didn't come and the weather was getting pretty bad. I got into my car with sue and we rode to where I knew they would be. As we approached the rode was blocked off by police and fireman. No one was allowed down that road. Luckily, Alex had already come out and was coming onto the highway to start home. When we got home and he was telling us about the tornado he said they could see it on land and they were racing it in the boat from the water. They had caught a big old catfish and they threw it into our fifty five gallon fish tank with my big Oscar. He wasn't in there long before I was taking him to a stream to set free. They were good days before I started to work. I wish I never went to work but as I said before, I knew the marriage was ending and I needed to support myself and three children, so off to work I unhappily went.

First I went to nursing school for three years and then I started working. The experience and credits that I got from college helped me land a job with the state, supposedly a dream job because of the benefits and the fifteen paid vacation days a year and the fifteen paid sick days a year.

One day I was at work and Sue called to tell me that Roxanne had gotten out of the back yard and bitten the next door lady on the leg. Her son was always tormenting Roxanne through the fence. We had a big six foot wooden stockade fence. The lady was talking to Sue at the door telling her the dog was out and Roxanne snuck up from behind her and bit her leg. I know now that she was protecting Sue. When Sue called me I asked her if the bite was bad. Sue replied that she couldn't tell because there was too much blood. I called the lady and offered to take her to the hospital and pay the bill but she declined. That night while I was fixing dinner the husband came over and knocked at the door. When I answered, he started yelling and screaming at me. We had words and he went home. I made sure that gate to out yard was secured at all times from then on. Eventually the family moved to Pennsylvania. This happened around the time I was diagnosed with Ulcerative Colitis and I was hospitalized for eight days with it. No one paid any attention to Roxanne and I was the one who fed her and took care of her and now I had been sick for months so we took her to the Humane Society. I will regret that until the day I die. She was a member of our family but I couldn't have her attacking people every time they came near one of us. Once at a park we were sitting on a bench and a boy on a skateboard zoomed past us and Roxanne lurched at him. I don't think she reached his leg but I left that park in a hurry. About a year or so before she was taken to the society association we bred her and she had a litter of nine pups. They were all so adorable I wanted to keep them all. The children really enjoyed having them while we had them, also. I found good homes for all of them and the new owners kept in touch and sent me e-mails showing me things the dogs were doing and how they were living.

Every summer I would be in the pool with the children and they were so spoiled because we were always boating and doing things. My mother and sister would come over to get in the pool. This was probably the happiest time of my life. We took my mother and drove to the mountains in upper New York state to visit my sister. I saw a Giant moose head in the back of someone's pickup truck going down the freeway. We went through New York City and went to the top of the Empire State Building and looked down at all the small people. I took a lot of pictures. One day we took Joey, his friend, and three month old Anthony to Longwood Gardens in Pennsylvania to see the flowers and giant goldfish. We made a good day of it, altogether. The flowers were very beautiful and extraordinary.

It didn't last long. In the spring of nineteen eighty six Alex and I were installing a storm door on the back of the house. We had only been living in the house nine and a half months. I could hear fire whistles blowing off in the distance. The phone rang around eight thirty and when I answered it my girlfriend, who lived on the street behind my mom, said my mother's house was on fire. I asked her if it was bad and she said she couldn't tell. She said a lot of black smoke was coming out of it. Alex and I let Joey, who was now fourteen, watch Sue and we took Anthony with us. The street going up to my childhood home was blocked off by fire trucks and police. A row of cars sat motionless on that street. I got out of our car and started running to my house, jumping over fire hoses along the way. I passed my dad sitting in his truck with the door opened and I yelled, "Where's mom?" He just shook his head. I continued on to the house. About a hundred people stood around a yellow crime scene tape. A bruiser of a female firefighter walked out the front door and went down the sidewalk. I yelled, "Where's my mom?" She just ignored me. I was devastated. I wanted to die. My mother and I were together every day except for that fatal day. We used to go to the flea markets, yard sales and have lunch and just hang out until the husbands came home from work. I stayed in a deep depression for three years then I remembered my mother had said she wished one of her girls was a nurse. She died in that fire and I knew she was depressed. Every day I went over there and she would cry because my dad and my sister met at the local club and drank until my mom was asleep. June nineteen eighty nine off to the community college I went for Registered Nursing. Not for me, for my mom. I also knew the marriage was going to end the same way they always end and I would need skills to get another job. I sent the kids to school, took care of the housework, and studied. Alex acted like he was jealous of what I was doing. He always said I was competing with him. Of course there was no competition. He dropped out of school in the seventh grade and I have three years of college. I never finished nursing. I dropped out on Valentine's Day nineteen ninety two. I just woke up one morning and said "this isn't for me". If my mom was alive she would have gotten me through it. She would have been my support system. Instead, I quit two weeks before graduation. Within a month I got a job as a clerk at a credit union. I stayed there part time and that is when we bought the thirty thousand dollar boat. After ten months working there I had a message on my answering machine when I got home from work one day. It was a state run nursing home. The lady told me that I was in their system as a Registered Nurse and she had a charge nurse job she wanted me for. I had to tell her I was not a nurse but if she had clerical jobs available I could do that and it just so happened that they needed a ward clerk. She told me where to go to put the application in, take the test, and get on the list of qualified candidates. Then when I got on the list, she hired me. I worked that job while putting in applications for better paying state jobs. At least now I had health coverage for me and all of my children. Alex used the Veteran's Hospital. After working in a state run nursing facility and watching every day how the nursing assistants treated the patients I made a living will and had it state "Never put me in an institution or facility". They were treated badly by the employees. One eighty something lady was punched and had black and blue marks on her. A nursing assistant did this. He was fired, of course. Finally one night when I went home from work I had a message to call a lady at a service center. I called and she said she wanted me to interview for Social Worker at the service center. I was ecstatic. The head Nurse at the nursing home pretended she was my supervisor and when the call came for a reference the head nurse gave me a great reference. I got hired and was so happy. The first thing I did was celebrate with a jug of homemade grape wine that I had made from my grape vines. I normally don't drink alcohol so you can imagine I was pretty sick the next day.

When I started the job the first thing that I did was buy a brand new, off the floor nineteen ninety four Mercury Cougar, black with a tan ragtop and a luggage rack. I had the car four months and someone slammed into it. Then a year later someone slammed into it again and it had over ten thousand dollars' worth of damage and the insurance company would not total it. Sue and I were taken to the hospital in ambulances, however, we were okay. I was hot. I worked as a social worker at the service center from June nineteen ninety four through October nineteen ninety seven. During this time I determined eligibility for food stamps and welfare checks and Medicaid. I was known as a worker who would do anything to help the people get what they needed. People that weren't even in my caseload were coming in asking for me. I loved helping the people and I think I'd still be there if I didn't get divorced. While there I saw people that I went to school with. Some were in sad situations. One man was withdrawing so bad for drugs that he could not finish the interview. He left and went out to the nearby motel and got a fix then came back and finished the interview. The stories that I heard were horrible. I felt badly for these people. One of my clients had a six year old son and was divorced. Her ex-husband drove for a cement company and made excellent money, yet my client never received any child support. One day a friend of mine who worked with her husband was telling me things about the man and he told me that the man was working using his son's social security number. Well, that explained why there was no child support. The next time my client came in I told her and she went straight to his job and raised the roof. Later he came into the service center hotter than hades and wanted to see me. My supervisor escorted him out and made co-workers walk me to my car when I went out for lunch. They did not let me go anywhere alone until things simmered down. After that the county police came and talked about installing security cameras at the service center. While the officer was talking to us in the meeting room he got a call on his radio and had to leave. Five minutes later my supervisor called me out and said to go home, my home had been robbed and the police were there.

When I pulled into the driveway the officer who was having our work meeting was standing on my lawn. People were putting black fingerprint dust all over the inside of my home. I had come home for lunch and when I left to go back to work the drug addict boy must have been watching and he came in the unlocked back door. He did not know that my twenty six year old son, Joey, was coming home for lunch right after me. My son walked in the front door and saw someone go out the backdoor. He thought Anthony and Sue were cutting school so he ran after them and saw that it was someone dragging our laundry basket with Joey's safe in it and a back pack filled with other goodies. Joey chased him with an ornamental sword I kept on the wall but the robber jumped the fence and ran through the yards. Joey said he thought that he recognized him from the neighborhood. Eventually the boy was caught months later after he had robbed eight different places including construction sites. Joey did know who he was from the neighborhood and said he was a drug addict. The boy was ordered to pay restitution to all of the people he robbed after he got out of jail and I was one of eight so I wasn't looking for restitution soon. It took ten years before that boy paid me and the others the restitution. Our homeowner's coverage reimbursed everything but all my gold jewelry and wedding rings were gone. My fingers had swollen and the rings were in my jewelry box. I had a lot of fine jewelry and never saw it again. A tiger's eye ring I had given Joey on his birthday was also taken. When the reimbursement check came it was for four thousand dollars. I ordered a six foot sub and had it delivered to my job and treated everyone in the building to lunch. I'm like that. Things settled down and work continued. Every day we were bombarded with people needing help. It was never ending.

{6}

One year after starting at the service center the stress caused me to have Ulcerative Colitis. I continued to work but it was hard. Many times I did not have control of my bowels. I missed a lot of days of work and in the middle of July, on my birthday, I was hospitalized for eight days on IV's. The Dr. told me that if I didn't get my stress under control that it would turn to cancer in about five years. Besides the stress from the job I had the stress from a husband who did not bother with me or talk to me and two children who were constantly starting arguments and violent fights with each other. They could not even look at each other without starting a n argument by saying something smart to each other. That was in nineteen ninety five. Today it is twenty fifteen and I retired this past October to get away from the stress. The children have grown up and I live with a Rottweiler who is my best friend. After thirty two years of breaking up violent fights with knives and guns I am finally almost stress free. Co-workers were having strokes right around meat my current job. It was getting bad. I would take people to food closets to get food., to hidden battered women homes, and to jobs to get the employment form completed for the benefits. I really did go above and beyond. I always got "distinguished" on my performance reviews. It was at the service center that I met back up with Charlie. You remember him, he's the one who rode my first husband around with a girl in the back seat and flipped his car. I always liked Charlie, especially when I was twelve and just starting to notice boys. Alex had his girlfriend and wasn't coming home at night so I started going out with Charlie. We lasted pretty long. He moved to the beach house with us but he couldn't stand it because he couldn't find work out in the middle of nowhere. The chicken plants were close by and you always smelled burnt chicken feathers. He liked crabbing and would set crab traps in the bay, but one day I came home from work to find a note saying he couldn't find a job down there and he was all alone during the day and back up north he went. A couple years went by and I heard he was HIV positive. I hurried and got tested like five times and was always negative so I think he was exposed to it after he left my trailer at the beach. He died in two thousand five . It took him fast. Good ole Charlie. Anthony and Sue both liked him a lot. We took him to Disney Land with us for that week and we had an argument out in the middle of no man's land and while he was in the store I left him. The kids said, "Mom aren't you going back?" I said "No" and kept on going. Charlie's sister lived in Sanford, Florida and he just had to call her. When I got back home to Delaware he called and we talked and one night I called him he wasn't there. His sister didn't say where he was. He was on a bus coming back to Delaware to surprise me and he told her not to tell me. It was early in the morning and someone was coming thru my door and when I saw him it was the greatest feeling. We had a lot of good times together but a lot of arguments, also. He was a Scorpio sign and they are rather argumentive. My vacation was coming to an end. I had taken a month off and had about a week left.

When I went back to work I put an application in for Senior Social Worker. I was swamped with clients and work. I didn't even have time to go to the bathroom. All of the other African Americans were just standing around talking and eating and joking. No one seemed to be doing any work except me. I didn't say anything. I just thought I was being prepped for the senior position I had put in for. NOT. We had weekly meetings in the supervisor's office every Friday. One Friday at the meeting the supervisor was telling everyone all this new work they were going to have to start doing, work that I had been doing. All of the workers started complaining and whining about it. The supervisor told them to be" quiet, they were going to do it, Jane had been doing it and now they were, too." One older African worker asked the supervisor, "Now why has Miss Jane been doing this work and we haven't?" The supervisor leaned across her desk and looked at them. She looked exactly like a black Grinch. She told them, "Because she is white and we are black and I was giving the black people a break." No one said anything. I stewed about it all weekend. On Monday morning two of the older workers and I had to go to Dover for a training class. I sat in the middle of them. I finally asked the older man if the supervisor discriminated against me on Friday. Without even looking up from his paper he said, "Yep, uh huh, she sure did." The three of us continued to discuss this atrocity and the instructors asked us to come out in the hall and let them in on things. We <u>were</u> causing quite a disturbance. We explained to the trainers what was going on and they took it from there. They had an investigation done. Everyone in the office was called to the main office to be interviewed and recorded. After all was said and done all the supervisor had to do was take a diversity class, and have a mentor. I was so stupid. I should have sued the state for discrimination!

Work continued as usual. After a while the supervisor and I became friends. It was strange to say the least. She treated me right and everyone pulled their share of the workload, not just me. My colitis was still bad. I had blood in my bowels and they were white with mucous. If I felt like I had to go I had to get to the bathroom yesterday, that's how bad it was. While I was seeing Charlie, John was coming around. Charlie was jealous of John, but they <u>were</u> good friends. He <u>did</u> have him in his car twenty four years ago with a girl <u>knowing</u> he was married to me. I finally broke up with Charlie and just concentrated on working and taking care of me and my two kids. Joey was twenty six; he basically took care of himself. I just provided the roof over his head. Alex worked at a used car dealership as a mechanic in the city of Stanton, a twenty minute drive from our home. When the children were about three and four Alex said he wasn't happy and wanted a divorce. I managed to talk him out of it for the sake of the children, but he had a girlfriend and I didn't find out until years later after he married her. We stayed together but Alex did not talk to me. He slept on the sofa for three years. This was years before I met up with Charlie. We were living in the same house but we weren't living together. He worked from seven until after eleven at night. During this time, John, (Joey's father and my life's love) started coming over and we would drive Anthony to his football practice and while he was practicing we would take Sue for a Happy Meal at McDonald's and just ride around having a good time. We did this a couple times a week for football practice and other days John would just come over and hang out. Why not? My husband wasn't around anymore and I thought that John and I were just being good friends and that was it. I <u>did</u> know he wasn't coming to visit Joey. He was twenty six and always gone somewhere with his friends. John had to go have double bi- pass surgery and he was afraid. He called me to come see him before he went. Charlie went too. He was really nervous about this surgery, but he came through it fine. He would call me four o'clock in the morning and all hours because of anxiety attacks. I would talk to him until he felt better. One early Sunday morning, at the beginning of summer (June twenty second), the phone rang. Joey got up out of bed to answer it. I saw his face and then he started crying and I knew it was his dad. He had heart failure the night before. He left Joey everything. Joey buried him and at the funeral parlor a lot of our old friends were coming up to me and saying, "John told us that you were getting back together". I thought we were just being civil to each other. I never knew. There goes another best friend. First my mom leaves me and now John leaves me. At the little wake I never felt more alone than I did that day. Joey had taken a picture of me not knowing and years later he showed it to me and said "You look like you just lost your best friend". I replied, "I did". Now life was just a motion. A thing we had to do. I felt like a robot without any emotion going through me. The great sadness came for a long time. Joey cleaned out his father's condominium and put all his furniture in storage. He came home one day and handed me an envelope. He said, "Here, this was taped to the back of dad's dresser." It was all of our wedding pictures and some of when Joey was small. I thought to myself, "Did he love me all those years?" "Why would he have these taped in his bedroom?" My heart was ripped right apart.

{7}

Alex and I continued like we always had. This was no way to live a life. We would go boating to a canal house on the river and eat lunch and drink a couple of drinks. Boating was always fun and lifted my spirits. Just to be around water lifted my spirits. I'm a water person, Cancer, and that's why we bought a house with an in ground pool. We did things because of the children, not with each other. We barely spoke to one another. I definitely felt unwanted. The Memorial Day weekend when we first bought the boat we drove it down the Delaware River to the Park to see Alex's boss and his family. We stayed overnight and started back the next morning, trying to beat a Nor'easter that was coming behind us. We didn't make it. We got as far as the Coast Guard station in Lewes and had to tie off and spend the night in the storm on the boat. Alex, Sue and Anthony slept down below. I was a nervous wreck and sat up top awake all night. The boat rocked from side to side hitting the wooden pile driver posts. I thought, I will never go boating with him again. But I did. The next day his boss lent us a car to get home and Alex and his boss went and got the boat a few days later. One fourth of July we drove up the Delaware to Penn's landing to watch the fireworks from the water. We were going to anchor there and come home in the morning. The mud would not hold the anchor and we kept drifting. After the fireworks were finished we started for home. As soon as we started to go the propeller hit something and we could go no faster than 5 miles an hour. Also we were lost. It was 3:00 in the morning and Alex would not admit that we were lost. I got on the CB radio and called out a mayday to get the coast guard's attention. Alex was mad, but I didn't care. It was late, I was tired and my children were asleep in the bottom of the boat. I wanted to go home! The Coast Guard came on board and checked for life jackets and flares. I could see Alex getting madder by the second. We did not tell them the children were asleep below because they didn't have their jackets on and we would have been in a lot of trouble. They directed us to our dock and then we went home and didn't speak to each other for days, maybe months. It was not uncommon for us to have an argument and then not speak to each other for months. We had a lot of good times going boating until one day Alex and I got into an argument and he yelled at me, "The boat's all I have!" I was taken aback. What were the children and I?

One day my children and I saw their father's boat parked near our dock but not at it. He had his girlfriend on it. They were nowhere around. They were probably in one of the restaurant/pubs on the canal. It really set in now that the marriage was over. It usually is when other people become involved. Still, we continued to live together. He didn't know that I knew about the girlfriend until Anthony overdosed on my colitis medication and I went to look for his dad. I found him at the airport lounge, leaning on the bar staring into some sixty plus year old woman's eyes. I told him what Anthony had done and he was in the car and wanted to see him and wanted him to come home. Alex came out to see Anthony but only for five minutes. He acted like he didn't care. He went back into the bar. Many times Anthony and Sue tried to over dose because of the divorce and I alone would rush them to the emergency room and stay with them all by myself. It was killing me to see them like this.

Finally the day before our fourteenth anniversary we were divorced (January sixteenth, nineteen ninety seven). I never saw such pain, suffering and devastation in anyone as I did in my children. Both children tried to kill themselves. Before the divorce was final I told Alex I didn't want the divorce (I initiated) because I could not stand to see what it was doing to our children. He said, "Well I do". It's that girlfriend. During the divorce he said I could have the house and I said he could have the boat. We had a notarized paper saying this. I kept the house for two years then Alex's new girlfriend, Jezzy got him a lawyer and made me either buy him out or sell the house and split the profit. I could not find my notarized letter anywhere to show the judge. I sold the house to Joey for just what was owed on it and no one got a dime.

{8}

We moved September thirtieth, nineteen ninety seven to my doublewide on the bay. I took a day off of work to get a U-Haul and ended up being an extra in a movie that a talk show host was producing in our city. She is very big and now has her own TV channel network. I met a famous movie star who must have been seven feet tall. My son was furious when I came home after filming. Joey went and got the U-Haul and packed it and moved me and his sister and brother two hours away the next morning. You never saw three such devastated people and this was the beginning of nearly a lifelong nightmare. For a month I drove two hours to work at the service center and two hours home. Then someone tapped my bumper at a red light and my Dr took me out of work and said I couldn't drive more than twenty five miles. The state transferred me to a service center half an hour from our beach home. My two teenagers had to make new friends. This was terrible. We were so far away from what family the children and I had left. Every time a pine cone fell out of a tree you could hear it tumble down the roof of the trailer. I am not a trailer person. I am used to houses and apartments. We had a big black German shepherd named "Shane". He had a heart murmur and a thyroid problem. He only lived to be two years old. He is buried under a tree next to my old doublewide at White House Beach on the bay. He was a great dog.

After the summer was over everyone left and went back to their homes for the winter. Sue would break into the empty trailers. She would get into the mailboxes that were lined up at the end of each street and once she stole someone's box of blank checks out of the mailbox. She wrote one to herself and signed her real name. I was so afraid she was going to get caught that I buried the checks and whisked her off to Florida and out of the state in case anyone was looking for the check thief and forger. For 32 years I lived a living hell trying to raise two bi-polar children while I myself was bi-polar/ major manic depressive. Both Sue and Anthony were bi-polar/manic depressive and Sue was also borderline personality disorder. None of us knew this at the time and no one was on any medication. So many times I wanted to commit suicide to escape the hell I was living day to day. We were pretty much left with not very many people in the park. In November we would awake in the morning to the sound of shot guns. Hunters would be in little boats out on the bay shooting at geese. Then there was that awful burnt chicken feather smell coming from the chicken factories. That was a constant.

One evening I got a telephone call from my brother. He had left home when he got in trouble when he was seventeen. He was living in Jacksonville, Florida. He wanted me to come for a visit. At this time my Ulcerative Colitis was really active. I had a month's worth of vacation saved up, so I got a friend of my brother's (Charlie) and mine and we took my two children to Disney Land in Orlando. I stopped off and got my brother's wife and six year old daughter. I had cashed in fifty two one hundred dollar savings bonds for this trip. I had twenty six hundred dollars for us. We did the four day hopper pass at Disney Land. We rode through Pirate's' Cove, A Small World, and lots of other attractions. Cinderella's castle was under renovation at the time so we didn't get to go through there. Charlie and Anthony and Sue went in this elevator to the top of a haunted mansion and then it just dropped. It was too scary for me so I sat that one out. I never did so much walking as I did at Disney Land. It got so I was looking for rides where you sat down for them. I really enjoyed the rain forest attraction. We saw everything we could see in four days and then I was ready to go home. We went back to my brother's. While there I met one of my brother's friends who is a drummer and I really liked him. We came home at the end of our vacation but my colitis never let up.

{9}

A year later my brother called and was very upset. His wife had died of a rare bone cancer and he kept saying "they took my daughter". I could not get a straight answer from him as to "who" took his daughter. It was President's Day weekend, so I took my children to their father's and girlfriend's house and told them I was going to Florida to help my brother. I got to Florida and learned that it was the" Department of Children and Families" that took his daughter. Apparently he was not the best dad. I was shocked. I told him, "You expect me to go up against them?" Have no fear Jane- I did just that. I stayed all week and ended up before a judge getting temporary custody of my niece. My brother wasn't allowed near her but no one told me. I brought her back to Delaware and we drove for two hours to my ex-husband's to get my children. Then we all went home to our trailer on the bay. We had a wonderful summer, me working and the kids clamming, crabbing and just playing in the bay. This was the same bay that my father brought me to as a child. The old cottage used to be directly across the bay from where we now lived. After about two months my brother came to stay with me. He got a job working on the fancy rich ocean front houses. He had no one except us. After living in Delaware for six months a person automatically becomes a resident of that state. During the fifth month the Children and Families people wanted to come do their home study which is procedure before allowing permanent custody. They lied to me. They told me they were sending my niece back to Florida because my brother was in the house. I didn't know anything. No one had ever told me any of this or I would have followed procedure. My six year old niece didn't have anyone in Florida! They put her in a foster home. She stayed there all summer until I finally got through to my brother to get a lawyer and go get her. When my niece heard them say they were sending her back to Florida she started crying and jumped in my arms and held me around my neck. Children and Families literally pried her from me. I can still see Sue and me standing in our driveway while my niece cried and waved goodbye out the back windshield. It took my brother three months to get a lawyer then we were back to Florida to get my niece. My children stayed with their dad for a while. Before my brother got the lawyer I had gone back to Florida to see if I could get her back. The drummer had come back to Delaware with us and I had to take him home. My brother said he would take care of Sue an Anthony until I got back. Sue's birthday was coming up and I waited until after her birthday. I go her a cake and presents and filled the refrigerator and cabinets for my brother and children before I left. I really didn't want to go but I had to get the drummer back home to Florida and no one had any money to put him on a plane. We drove throughout the night and he drank his beer along the way and sang and talked excessively so that it got on my nerves. Finally, around eleven at night and going eighty miles down I 95 in North Carolina I couldn't take him anymore. I went to pull over on the shoulder. I didn't know that you were supposed to slow down first and then pull onto the shoulder. I pulled over going as fast as I was and lost control of the car. Over the guardrail and down and embankment we flew. The car was rushing at trees and I didn't have my seatbelt on. All I could think of were my children and how I was going to hit one of those trees and be killed. It looked like we were on a roller coaster with thousands of trees headed straight for us. I put my head down, closed my eyes, braced, and said, "Oh GOD". I felt this extraordinarily overwhelming feeling of peace and although

My eyes were closed I could tell there was a warm very bright light surrounding us. After a While I opened my eyes and the car had stopped but not hit any of the trees. My friend and I pushed the car so that we could drive out of the trees and back onto the road. We immediately stopped at the first gas station we saw. We pulled up to the gas pump and two men were standing in the store window looking at us and laughing. I got out of the car to see what was so funny and my car looked like we had it camouflaged with leaves and tree branches. It actually looked like we had just taken it out of hiding in the bushes. Tree sticks stuck out from all of the tires. Branches and leaves were all over the car. We fueled up and continued onto Florida. We arrived about eight o'clock the next morning. I went to a Winn Dixie grocery store to get something to eat. A little old woman was looking at the butter and I was so in awe and stunned that I told her my whole experience. She looked at me and said, "You know why you were saved, don't you?" I said, "No", and she said "it's because you called on the Lord at the last minute." I drove back to the house and that day, one by one my tires went flat from the sticks in them. They had broken the tire seals. I now wear St. Jude, St. Christopher and the Virgin Mary around my neck, and I am a true witness to the fact that everything we have been taught IS real. At first I thought it was GOD that saved us but now I am pretty sure it was a guardian angel, but I could be wrong. I got a job at a grocery store, worked long enough to get a first pay, then hauled it back to Delaware and my children.

Now came the job of getting my brother down there to get his child. We left at night and drove all through the night. Once I had to pee so we stopped on the side of the road and I went behind some bushes to go and slid down an embankment. I had to scream for my brother to come pull me up.

We arrived in Florida and my brother went into the Children and Families building while I waited outside. Off in the distance I saw two women and a little girl walking toward me. As they got closer and closer my niece kept looking at me. When they got close enough where she could recognize me she started running to me, screaming. She ran right in my arms and I swung her around and she said, "Aunt Jane, did you come to take me back to Delaware?" I said "Yes, I did. Your dad's inside now". We all drove home to my beach trailer and my brother and niece were living with us. While I was in Florida I started a relationship with my brother's friend. I made a deal with my brother. He was to live in my trailer while I went to Florida to look for a job and get a place to live so I could bring Sue and Anthony there. One day I received a call from Sue. My brother had left them and went to Maryland to stay with another sister. My children were home all by themselves! I called their father and asked him to go get them until I could get back up there. He immediately went into court and had his child support stopped and told them that I deserted my children. This was not true! I would die for my children. How dare he? I arrived back in Delaware and their father TOOK ME TO COURT and asked the judge to give me custody again, that he didn't want it. He didn't want it? He never was a father to them. I had sold the beach house and the three of us went back to where we came from. Joey didn't want us there. He had always been jealous of Anthony and Sue. He told me so, himself, many years later. He let me and Sue stay with him but not Anthony. I had to take Anthony to one of his friends to stay. This was terrible. It wasn't supposed to be this way. My family is all split up and all over the place. I couldn't stand it. I went to Anthony's friend's house and got him. Sue didn't want to go to Florida so she decided she was going to stay with my sister until I got a house. It was not a good idea for her to be at my sister's, but we didn't know it until later. Still Sue was adamant about not going to Florida.

{10}

Anthony and I drove to Florida with the clothes we could fit in the trunk. We got there and I tracked my brother down. He had left my niece with my sister and was living it up again in Florida. Anthony and I stayed with different friends of my brother's until I was able to find us a rent to own house. It was August. It had taken me four months to get a job and a place to live. I called Sue and sent her pictures of the house. Her father put her on a plane and midnight Anthony and I met her plane. She was having it bad when she wasn't with us. I was so happy to see her. I had really missed having her with me. I had never been away from any of my children for any amount of time, let alone four months! I didn't know how to act without all the fighting . I worked temp jobs and within a month I had gotten hired by a state agency. I was so happy that the three of us were back together again. We moved into that house and slept on the floor and a co-worker gave me a 13 inch black and white TV. We sat in beach chairs in the living room watching it. Hurricane Floyd was coming. The Eastern coast of Florida had to evacuate. Anthony looked at me and said "Aren't we going to evacuate?" I asked him where we would go. No one wanted us and that's why we came to Florida. The hurricane turned out to be nothing more than a rainstorm. Anthony put a green trash bag on and went out in it, only to have me yell to get back in the house. I told them, "If GOD means for us to die in an empty house in a hurricane in Florida, then that's what will happen". Sue enrolled in school, I worked and Anthony got a job at the grocery store. Little by little I put furniture and household items in that house. I was making another home. None of us were happy. We were just going through the motions. The three of us, all with bi-polar/manic depressive disorder were definitely NOT a good trio. I tried so hard to keep us sane, but Anthony ended up doing more drugs and I didn't like the looks of his friends. He and Sue were always fighting and stealing my Ulcerative Colitis medication and my back pain medication. No matter where I hid them somehow they managed to find them. They were violent fights and I had to get between them to break them up and try to protect Sue. Sometimes I thought if she just wouldn't be so smart mouth everything would be okay, but that went both ways.

I heard on the radio one morning on the way to work that extras were wanted for a movie called Tigerland, that part of it was being filmed in Starke, Florida. I took Anthony to audition and they chose him out of hundreds of teens and young adults. You had to be eighteen to be in the movie and Anthony was only sixteen. I fixed his birth certificate to say he was eighteen. I DO NOT recommend anyone doing this. I was on the road for three hours every morning before I got to work. At five thirty a. m. I had to have Anthony an hour away at the filming site. Then I came home and dropped Sue off at school and then I drove to work. Three hours every single morning for two months. Anthony met a very famous and well known director and ate lunch at the director's table with the stars of the movie. He shadowed the star, Colin Farrell. Anthony made a little over a thousand dollars for his role as an extra and Colin Farrell's shadow. He had a good memory for once, instead of just bad ones. We have the movie in our collection and you can see Anthony in a few places big as life.

One night, three months after the movie job ended, Suehad a girlfriend spend the night. They both slept on the living room sectional. Anthony came in at five o'clock in the morning from a night of partying. Sue said he got mad because she wouldn't give him a cigarette and this started a horrible fight. I heard the noise, woke up and came into the living room to see what was going on. The next thing I know, Anthony has a gun and is chasing Sue. I tried to grab the gun from him and we wrestled and the gun fell on the floor into two pieces. In the meantime Sue had dialed nine one one then changed her mind and hung up. I take the phone off the hook when we go to bed and the police got the answering machine. They came to the house to see if everything was okay. We had told Anthony to get in his room and we would get rid of them. The police made Sue and I come outside. We told them they had an argument and everything was okay now. They wanted to go into the house and we would not let them. They asked why we didn't want them to go into the house and Sueand I looked at each other back and forth and I said "because he has a gun". What the hell did I just do? This was my baby. I told him we would get rid of the police and here I just threw him to the wolves. How can I be so stupid? The one cop told the other one to put us in the back of the police car so we didn't get caught in the crossfire. I screamed "The gun is in two pieces. It's broken. I had it". They shoved us unwillingly into their car and then what seemed like millions of them came, shutting off our neighborhood and running around with guns drawn ready to shoot the first thing that moved. Anthony had managed to run out the back door and while the cops searched yards Anthony stayed hidden. He had just finished being an extra in the movie Tigerland. It was about Viet Nam. I think what Anthony learned in that movie helped him survive that day. Everyone was sure he was going to be Swiss cheese. Finally a cop came near my window and through the window I begged him not to shoot my son. He said he wanted to get married next month. I told him I worked for the state and I would not lie to him, the gun is broken. After a while Anthony came walking down our street like nothing is going on and the cops were yelling for him to lie on the ground and he yelled "No I'm not lying on the ground". He went to put his hand in his pocket and the cops really went ballistic screaming to get his hand out of his pocket. Thank GOD, he took his hand out. Then the cops started yelling to put his hands in the air and he told them "No", all the while walking to our house, up the stairs, and into the house. I never cried and prayed so much in my life for that child. In the meanwhile we could hear everything being said over the police car radio. We heard them say that they had Anthony on the phone and that "the negotiators were on the way, so have the mother ready. We're going to need her." Then they said the mother was not being very cooperative. If someone was out to shoot your child would you cooperate? No, you wouldn't be so stupid to get into this situation to begin with. Remember now, my bi-polar gives me problems with authorities. I know how the police are. Shoot first, ask questions later. Finally Sue said "What's he doing?" I looked up to see Anthony standing in our driveway pointing that broken gun at the swat team. I pray they believed me when I told them the gun was broken. They kept yelling at him to lie down and put the gun down. He was pointing it at them!!! I know GOD must have been there that day because finally Anthony put the gun down and he let them arrest him. This was all over an argument with his sister that I wasn't equipped to handle on my own. If you ever get divorced I beg you to have a father figure for your son. I learned in Nursing that age twelve is the most critical time for a boy to have his father. That's how old Anthony was when we separated. His father told him to take care of me. It is not a twelve year old's responsibility to take care of his mother. We could not make bail for a while but when we did Anthony showed me a golf ball sized lump near his groin. My nurse's training told me Cancer. I took him to Shands hospital for a biopsy. It would take a few weeks to get the results. I hired a lawyer and I told him about the biopsy and lump and he never told anyone. While Anthony was at the detention center my dad died. I went to the center and asked them to tell Anthony so that he didn't think I deserted him. My brother, Sue and I went to Delaware to go to my father's funeral, and then the next day I drove right back to Florida. The detention center never told Anthony and that's exactly what he thought; that I deserted him. He told me he thought I died and he was stuck there all alone. At sentencing Anthony received four years at an adult prison in Lake Butler, Florida. He was sixteen years old. I always think of that judge that brought him back and resentenced him.

One day at work the phone call came. My son has cancer. He has a fast growing type B non-Hodgkin's lymphoma. If he doesn't start treatment right away he only has a few months to live. I cried and all my co-workers came running. I called the Dr and asked them to fax me the paperwork saying Anthony has cancer and I immediately faxed it to the lawyer then called to make sure he got it. He went and told the judge, who should have been told in the beginning and the judge immediately called Anthony back from the adult prison and he had to go before the judge again. I will never forget that judge sitting up on his high bench saying, "If I would have known this young man was waiting for results from a biopsy I would have never sentenced him. He changed the sentence from four years in an adult prison to a year on house arrest with an ankle bracelet, followed by two years' probation. I could have hurt that lawyer. I paid him twenty five hundred dollars to help Anthony and the only one he helped was his self. Anthony had his first chemo treatment around October or November. I remember at Christmas we were opening presents and Anthony was sweating. He wiped his forehead and hair out of his eyes and when he took his hand away there was a lot of hair in his hand. He started to cry. This was the beginning of his losing his hair. All of his friends had their heads shaved and wore bandanas to make Anthony feel better. It worked. Anthony had never known anyone who had cancer before and he really didn't think anything was wrong with him. The nights before his chemo he would go out and drink alcohol and the next day I would have to cancel the chemo because they can't do it with alcohol in your system. I finally made Anthony realize that he had a very serious illness. I had everyone I talked to praying for him. I asked people that I didn't even know, people at church, at work, everywhere. I believe in the power of prayer. Anthony had his last chemo in 2001, just before he graduated and he is now a cancer survivor. It has been fifteen years and he has survived cancer. It was a very hard thing to go through. The dr's had him on so many prescriptions while he was doing the chemo. He had marijuana pills, pain pills, anxiety pills, nausea pills, and others that I can't remember. When the chemo ended so did the prescriptions. The Dr's cut him off cold turkey. That was when Anthony started going out and getting drugs to self-medicate. For three months I barricaded the door so that he couldn't get out, but he always did. One night he came home with his eye all bloody and the side of his face bashed in. He had gone to get drugs and got into a fight with the main drug dealer and two of his friends. He could have been killed. I wrestled him every night to try to keep him inside and alive and he always got out. Finally I could no longer do it without help. I telephoned his probation officer lady and explained things to her. She said she had been waiting for it. She said she knew he would want drugs after the Dr's cut him off. I was so relieved. I had help at last. She was very understanding. I stayed out of it and let her do her job. Anthony was supposed to be on house arrest and she would let him go to his friend's house to roast oysters on the grill, "after she left". She knew of my plan to go back home and she helped get the probation transferred to Delaware after the house arrest was over.

Before he got the help from his probation officer one night he called 911 and told them to come get him, they know where he lives. I hurried and we all left the house before the police arrived. Then Anthony took off and I couldn't find him. I drove down our street looking for him and half a dozen police men were all over our front yard and stairs. I think they even went into the house. I kept on driving and ended up two blocks away at a friend's house. She and I saw Anthony walking up the street and we hurried and grabbed him and got him into her house until the police left. After a while I went home and gave the police a lame excuse about him, the cancer and the drugs. I told them that his probation officer was helping him. They bought it and left. Sue was spending the night with her friend that night. One night I came home from a friends' and Sue looked very upset. I asked her what was wrong and she would not tell me. I kept asking and finally she told me that she was talking on the phone to one of her friends and Anthony wanted to use the phone and because she wouldn't give it to him he put a gun to her head. I flew into him. I didn't know he had a gun again. I got in his face and pushed him and told him to point that gun in my face. I really let him have it and I know I should have done that years ago. That child needed to respect me and what I said and neither of them did. Having children exactly 13 months apart was proving not to be any fun as they became older. I could not take much more of this living hell. One other day he was walking down Main Street and he waved a gun at one of his enemies and the boy went home and called the police and told them where Anthony and the gun were. The police came to frisk Anthony but before they got to him he threw the gun in a patch of woods. He said the police looked all over for it but they never found it. They left Anthony alone and moved on. I got Sue and met Anthony on Main Street and he showed us where he threw the gun. We looked and looked but we could not find it. Surely the police would be back to look and Anthony would be in jail again. Finally Sue found the gun lying on some leaves and I drove the three of us up over a bridge that crosses a river and made Anthony throw the gun in the river. I told him he better never get another one.

One night I got a telephone call from one of Jessica's friends. She said that Jessica was running up and down Main Street trying to get hit by a car over some boy. I rushed down the three blocks to Main Street and put my car in park and got out to get her. I had a hard time getting her in the car but I managed. She was in bad shape, over this boy. I got her home and talked to her, trying to make her feel better and cheer her up. She scared me because she was always trying to hurt herself. If she and Anthony weren't hurting each other they were hurting themselves. We got over the boy.

While we were living in Florida and going through all the drama, the three of us were attending Community College at Jacksonville. Anthony and Sue were going for diplomas and I took a psychology class and a humanities class. The three of us went to class at the same times. Anthony got his diploma and there was a big ceremony for graduation. He didn't want to go because he had just had his last chemo and didn't feel well. I talked him into it because it was a once in a lifetime event. He marched down the aisle and up onto the stage to get his diploma and a white dove flew from the rafters and landed at my feet. I told Sue to look. "It's a sign". I silently thanked GOD for letting us be where we were. Sue ended up getting her diploma when she moved back to Florida. She then went to college for crime scene investigator. She was a few months away from her master's when she decided to write a book about her violent life.

On a good night I would go out with my drummer boyfriend. We would go to clubs and he would play the drums in the band and when they were on break he would come sit with me. All of our friends would go too, and dance the night away. When I left Florida to come home to Delaware I left him behind. Thirteen years later he still keeps in touch with me. He has been living in Las Vegas on Tropicana Boulevard with his eighty six year old mother. He goes to the clubs in Vegas and plays the drums with the bands there. He keeps trying to get me to come out there, but after Florida I don't want to leave the house. I have yelled at him so many times for calling me in the middle of the night. Vegas is three hours behind Delaware.

While still in Florida we would go to the Beach and to the Plantation. The Plantation road was actually cut through the trees by the slaves over a hundred years ago. They lived in little rooms built out of oyster shells with tiny windows. The Plantation owner's mansion is now a museum. It is a bit of history that saddens you to see.

We never went to Disney Land or any of the other Florida attractions the entire three years that we lived there. I was always working and then Anthony was sick with Cancer. We had already been to Disney years before, anyway.

Jacksonville is a Navy city. Mayport is the place where all of the Navy people live. Jessica had a friend that lived there. That is the closest I ever got the Navy, except for my dad. I never told my father. I'm sure he would have told me to quit working in the welfare office and get into the Navy, but at this point I think I was too old. My drummer would also take us out to Mayport to look at the big Navy ships. Today my son Joey is the lead mechanic who fixes the gears on those ships.

At the Florida/Georgia state line there is a flea market called Pecan Park. It is one of the largest flea markets I have ever seen. I brought a lot of wall pictures and items back from there and that is also where we bought our dog, Max. I took the kids up there every weekend almost when I had extra money. Bi-polar people spend money on impulse when not on medication, and none of us were on medication. Most of the time I spent riding around looking for a better place to live. We were on a particular street and it was slowly going to the dogs. I got approved for a mortgage to buy the house we were living in right around the time that Anthony started losing his hair. I never signed the contract and told the landlord that I was in no condition to buy a house at that time. I knew I was going back to Delaware, I just didn't know when. I didn't tell him I was going back up north so he said he understood and could wait until I was ready to buy the house. That proved to be never. It was a cute little house with a very large back yard. One of the neighbors gave me a small electric lawn mower. We had a palm tree in the front yard, which meant Palmetto bugs. Their giant flying roaches. We had a heat pump so the electric for heat and air conditioning was reasonable. We only had two bedrooms, though. Sue and I had to share a room. I didn't mind. I don't know if she did or not. I wasn't about to open a can of worms. We had a driveway, but the garage was falling down and actually needed to be torn down. You could not use it and it was dangerous to go near. It did not get torn down until after we moved out.

One night I awoke to a lot of noise in the living room. I went out to see what was happening and Sue had a can of bathroom cleaner and was spraying a poor Palmetto bug. Another time, just before we came back to Delaware, a bird flew down our fireplace and was stuck in a vase. I took the vase outside and turned it upside down and the bird flew away. Yes, it was a cute little house and we loved the fireplace but it was ten minutes from a Stadium and not in a good area. We started to go to church at a little church around the corner from us. The pastor was a young man from England and he and his wife had just had a baby. Sue, Anthony and I enjoyed going to that church. We would have covered dish suppers and the people were so friendly. One Christmas I got a Christmas card with a hundred dollar gift card and it was signed Santa. I was sure it was from someone at the church. They gave us a welcome basket when we first moved in. People don't do that up north anymore. The people in northern Florida called us "damned Yankees" and other northerners "snow birds". They wished the north would stay up north. Well I knew of three people that were headed north, never to come back.

In my work place, if you are a good worker and meet high standards you are rewarded with a cash bonus. It could range from fifty dollars to seventeen hundred and fifty dollars. I got the seventeen hundred and fifty dollars and immediately got the probation transferred to

Delaware and got a U-Haul with a trailer for Anthony's car. I gave two weeks' notice at my job and loaded that U-Haul and got out of there as fast as I could. We lived there for three years exactly in that nightmare. We had no family there. My brother had taken off for Louisiana or somewhere and it was just us. All of our family was back in Delaware. I had a problem with Sue. She didn't want to go home but she wasn't going to be 18 for three more months. First she didn't want to come to Florida and now she doesn't want to leave. It's my fault. Since we had to give up our home with Joey I dragged my children all over the East Coast. Up and down. Down and up. I needed help, but there was none. Their father was nonexistent in their lives. When we told him that Anthony had cancer it was as if he didn't care. He never paid child support to help with the medications. Sue ran away. I had to report her missing and track her down. She came home with us, but at eleven o'clock p. m. the night before she turned eighteen I was standing at a bus station in Wilmington waving bye to her. She was going back to Florida and she was eighteen and I couldn't stop her. When we were leaving Florida Anthony drove the U-Haul with his German Shepherd, Max, riding in the passenger seat, while towing his car. Once along I 95 he motioned for us to pull over and we did. The he ran back to tell me something and Max jumped out of the U-Haul's driver's window to go after Anthony and was hanging from the truck because the leash had caught on something. We got him safely back in the truck and Anthony didn't stop any more unless he put the window up. We had a time driving almost nine hundred miles home, but by the grace of GOD we made it in one piece. The furniture was put into storage and this is when the three of us started staying wherever we could. Sue went back to Florida and struggled for ten years down there. She always called me for money and I always Western Unioned it. One day she called me and asked if I could send her money to get a new license. I asked where her old license was and she said that she had gone out drinking with friends the night before in their truck and lost her pocketbook. She said they threw her out of the truck into a ditch and left her. I'm surprised she wasn't killed, yet still she would not come home. I sent money to fix her car, to help get electric and water turned on, when she needed food, you name it. She did not want to come home because of Anthony. He continued to get into trouble and I continued to pay lawyers and bails. It was a nightmare. Finally she came home. The violent fighting continued and Anthony's' crime record just grew and grew. Their father was nonexistent. I later found out that he left a first wife and 4 children on Christmas Eve. He told them he was going to Delaware to see his mother and grandmother and never went back. He has children showing up from everywhere. A lady in her 40's came all the way from Thailand to see what her father looked like. He had gotten her mother pregnant while he was on R & R. I married a dog. I raised Joey to be a fine upstanding community figure but I had my mom and dad's help. Anthony never had a father figure. I cannot stress the importance of having an appropriate father figure for your son, mainly at twelve onward. Children need both parents. There should be a law against single mother's having children. Trying to survive life while being bi-polar, manic depressive, and not knowing it is scary, especially with three in the same house. All three of us should have been on Bi-polar/manic depressive medication. Life might have turned out a lot different and better.

{11}

I went to work every day, taking off for one crisis after another. My supervisor told me she didn't know how I wasn't having a breakdown. I told her I didn't have time. Anthony was in jail. He was out. Sue moved in with her father. She moved back home. I wasn't strong enough to raise two kids. I needed help, but there was never any to come. Both of my parents were dead and I had no friends. I had alienated all my friends for Alex. He was very cold and thought he was better than everyone else. He treated my mom bad because she drank beer and here he was drinking mixed drinks. I walked around like a zombie. I'm strong, so they say, but I couldn't handle this situation!

When we got to Delaware from Florida my youngest brother let us stay with him until I got on my feet. There was a revolving door and he blasted music at three o'clock in the morning knowing I had to get up and go to work. He was jealous of Anthony and picked a fight with him and one of my brother's neighbor's that didn't like him called the police. They both spent the night in jail and now Anthony has broken probation in Florida. For fifteen years Delaware has been trying to get Florida to take my son and for fifteen years Florida keeps telling Delaware "No". I wish they would all just leave him alone.

Anthony and Sue went to live with their father. I stayed in my car parked next to my mom and dad's grave. Sometimes I slept up on a hill at the Park before it got cold. I was back and forth from Joey's to my brother's. Joey had a girlfriend who didn't want me living there. My brother's house had too much traffic and I was afraid to be there. Anthony and Sue's father left his girlfriends' house to get an apartment for his children. They were row apartments and a prostitute lived right next door to them. It killed me to have my children here. To think we went from a good life to this!

I worked Temp agency jobs and finally I got rehired with the state sending out welfare checks and food stamps. Anthony was doing an apprenticeship and he got an apartment. We didn't stay there long before I rented a house. Anthony was still doing drugs and Sue was still living and struggling in Florida. One night I got into an argument with Anthony about the drugs. I told him to shape up or ship out. He called someone and said he didn't have to listen to this and left. At three o'clock in the morning he tapped on my bedroom window to let him in. I asked where his key was. He didn't know. People on drugs lose a lot of things and forget a lot of things. I let him in and told him I was going back to bed. He turned the TV on and got on the sofa. I was glad he was safe at home. I awoke around seven in the morning and the front door was wide open (in the middle of January) and Anthony was gone. There was a donut store behind us and I thought maybe he went to get coffee and donuts. The morning went on and he didn't come home. I really was worried now. Where is he? Finally, around two o'clock he telephoned me and said he was arrested about four thirty that morning for robbing the Wawa. I died. Not literally, but inside. All of me just collapsed. Robbery? I'm crying as I write this. Maybe this whole thing is my fault. Maybe it's not. I do know that I should have never stayed with his father or married him after he tried to strangle me and kicked me in the stomach when I was three months pregnant. I couldn't get Anthony bailed out until around July after I moved into a house behind my brother's house. While he was in jail I sued their dad for money he owed me that the judge awarded me in the divorce. I got it and rented the house behind my brother's.

The day I moved in two girls from across the street came over and wanted to help and be nosey. They were eighteen and seventeen. I told them no thank you. They found out that I used to be a Social Worker at the service center. The next thing I know my car has baby food and smashed eggs all over it. I didn't know it but they had been caught at welfare fraud at the old service center I used to work at, so they didn't especially like us people. The police said if you don't see them do it they can't help. Every single time I walked out my door to go somewhere the eighteen year old, who was nine months pregnant, yelled over at me, "I'm going to f --- you up". I ignored her because she was just a teen and I was over fifty. Ketchup was thrown all over my front steps. I just ignored her yelling and then Anthony came home on bail. Anthony stayed in jail until July when my aunt in Tennessee sent me bail money for him. I told him about this girl yelling these things at me and one day we lit the kerosene heater and smoke went up into the air. I opened the door and propped it with a flower pot. He saw the condition I was in and screamed that they were making me a prisoner in my own home. I was afraid to go outside. The girl was standing in her doorway, with no door, as usual, and she yelled her nasty threat at me. Anthony heard her and went on the step and yelled at her and asked her who she thought she was yelling at his mother. A large argument started and then a hillbilly pickup truck comes noisily up the road and stops at her house. A teen boy jumps out, grabs a clam rake, (the kind you use for clamming) and runs to hit Anthony on our property with it. Anthony went after him like there was no tomorrow and I jumped in between the other boy with the rake and Anthony. I was just walking in the house and got on the phone to call the police when the dispatcher tells me the police are out front. That girl that had been doing all these things to me from May to July has called the police. I don't believe the little so and so. The police woman walked over and told me to put the phone down. I told her "No, I'm talking to another officer". She got mad and tried to walk right into my home. I shut the door on her. Anthony got upset and kept saying he was going to go back to jail. I told him he wasn't. We walked out our back door and down the alley to my brother's house. The clam rake hillbilly saw us and screamed, "There they go now over to Sam Long's". Anthony ran in my brother's front door. He was shirtless. A huge policeman ran right after him but when he stepped up on the front step and yanked that locked screen door open I grabbed him by the scruff of his neck and pulled him backward. His microphone fell off. A policewoman got me on the ground and handcuffed me. All the police went into my brother's house. Anthony, shirtless, put his hands in the air and said don't shoot. They shot him anyway with the Taser gun. Anthony was squirming on the floor from the electrical volts. The police kept yelling at him to put his hands behind his back. He couldn't do it because he was paralyzed from the Taser. Because he could not put his hands behind his back the police started kicking him in the ribs and back. My brother stood up off his sofa and said, "Hey, wait a minute now". One of the cops told him to sit down and shut up or they would arrest him, too. Anthony and I both went to jail that night. The police had just finished processing me and was finding out what number cell to put me in when they were told I was bailed out. Joey had come and bailed me out at one o'clock in the morning. I had to go to my brother's to look for my keys in his yard. I found them and went home. I cried so hard and was in such shock that the girl across the street could do what she had done to me for months and then cause all this to happen to Anthony and I. Sue called. I talked to her for a while and then took seventy one Klonopin. Yes, I tried to overdose and commit suicide on benzodiazepines. I didn't know it wouldn't work. I woke up the next morning. I was mad! They took Anthony away and they tried to kill him in my eyes. I didn't want to live on this earth. I have to because I am all Anthony has. His father is not a constant for Anthony. Joey called the police because I tried to commit suicide. I was put in a psych ward and left there for a week. After I finally got out I got the bail for Anthony and got him out of jail. I filed a complaint directly with Internal Affairs but of course CYA and the police department do that better than any other organization. They were found to be justified in kicking a Tasered paralyzed person in the ribs over and over. I hate them. It's a Bi-Polar thing. Not long after this incident, Anthony was in the convenience store and his dad was in the car. The hillbilly and his friend jumped Anthony in the store. Anthony's dad saw them and ran in the store and you do not want an ex-Marine who has done 2 tours in Viet Nam after you. In January Anthony was sentenced to two or three years in jail for robbing the Wawa the previous January. I gave up the rental and moved back to my family home to keep my brother from losing it. He was three months behind on the rent and foreclosure was imminent. My dad wanted to keep that house in the family. It was a two story brick house and had been in our family for over fifty years. House sharks were after my brother to sell them the house for a hundred thousand dollars. Those houses were selling for over a hundred and eighty thousand dollars. He came and asked me to move in with him, pay rent and we could both live in our childhood home, not to mention saving it. I did just that. I paid off the bank and the sharks took a hike, except for one. He was a drug buddy of my brother's. His name was Bill and I didn't know it but he had a plan to get me back out of the house so he and his brother could easily get the house from my brother. First, he was my brother's friend and I knew that meant drugs were involved. No selling, using. My brother could smoke so much crack cocaine and drink so much beer that someone could slip a piece of paper under his nose and say sign and he would. I have seen him in a drunken, drug induced stupor. I tried to look out for him the best I could while I lived there but I couldn't put up with the nasty way he treated me. He was very belligerent and rude. I was paying his three hundred a month mortgage and his small electric bill while he slept on the sofa all day and partied all night. He rented a room to Bill. This was unbelievable. Then Bill slowly seduced me and my brother got mad and threw Bill out. Bill talked me into getting an apartment with him and every day at lunchtime I would bring boxes home and put them in my room. My brother was never home. Bill had to be out the following Friday. He brought a large truck and backed it into the driveway and started loading my entire thing s and his into the truck. My brother came to me and said, "I didn't tell you to get out. I told him." He had found a job and every day while I was bringing boxes he had been at work. I felt so bad. I made up a lame excuse and let Bill move me to an apartment. We weren't at the apartment two months before he was moving back into a room at my brother's house. I kicked him out because he told Sue that he wouldn't mind having sex with her. She had come back from Florida finally after ten years of struggling down there. Now I knew what he was doing. He was getting my brother so messed up on alcohol and drugs that he was going to get the house he wanted so bad to flip while I was no longer there in the way. My sister saw my brother at the shopping center and he told her he was selling the house to Bill's brother for seventy five thousand dollars. She told him that I would give him a hundred and twenty thousand for it. She said it seemed to go right over his head. He did not speak to me so I couldn't talk to him about the house myself. He acted so cold and mean to me. He just plain and simply did not want me to have our family home. It may have held bad memories for him, but it held good ones for me. He sold a hundred and eighty thousand house to his crack head drug buddy for his brother for seventy five thousand dollars. My dad wanted to keep it in the family. I did not hear from my brother until the twenty five thousand dollars that he cleared was gone and he was broke. He has been homeless and living in his truck for five years now. When he sold the house I cried and cried forever. At that moment I was determined to get out of that apartment. I was living in the apartment when Anthony got out of jail for the robbery charge. It wasn't long before somebody that he met in jail came around and introduced Anthony to his sister, Nina. Anthony started dating her and the first night he took her out she spent the night at our apartment. Then she was there the next night. Anthony said she didn't have anywhere to go. I said I didn't care, get rid of her. I came home from work one day and there was a pipe for marijuana and marijuana lying on my sofa. I told Anthony that she was going to end up getting him in more trouble. It took me a month to get her out of my apartment. Anthony continued to see her while going to massage therapy school. He graduated and got his diploma from there but he cannot practice as a masseuse because he has a felony on his record. Now he owes student loans. The school director knew Anthony had the felony and couldn't practice when he signed him up for classes. I'm trying to find someone to complain about this to. They should not have signed him up if they knew he'd never be able to work.

It was July and on January twenty ninth I moved into my own home. It was a fixer upper, but I've been making a home, again. The stress that the sellers put me through was unbearable that my doctor sent me for a cat scan because I was always having headaches. I have a brain tumor. It's small as a pea and not doing anything so we just watch it. Anthony got a job delivering pizzas. That lasted about two months then he got a job for another pizza place delivering. He was still seeing Nina and I am almost certain that he was sneaking her into my home while I was a t work. Anthony was spending the money that he was getting from the customers for payment for their pizzas. I had to give him money to keep him from getting arrested for theft. I knew he was doing pain pills and cocaine with Nina. She was a bad influence. When Anthony first came home from jail he was clean and not doing any drugs. Nina got him started back on them. She also introduced him to the seboxon clinic, which is discussed further in the story. I did not want him with this girl. She was bad news. Anthony got another job driving for another pizza place and one night he didn't come back from his delivery. The boss called me and wanted to know if he was at home. I told him No he wasn't and I drove to his work place. When I got there, Nina was sitting at the bar drinking with some man. I was told that Anthony was hijacked by gunpoint when he stopped at a red light and the robber stole all the money and made Anthony drive him to Philadelphia and took his car and left him walking home along I 95. He filed a police report. A day or two went by and we were notified that Anthony's car was in Chester and I drove him to Chester to get it. I had to pay the towing company a hundred and sixty dollars to get the car. Anthony continued to work at the pizza place for a while and then quit. Nina and drugs were all he was interested in. I did not like this life. Finally he got rid of her and saw her for what she was. She wanted to move in with someone but this boy lived with his mother. Anthony didn't have his own place or else she could have lived with him. I was not having her shacking up at my home. And I wanted no part of the drug scene and it was all I could do to try to get Anthony off of them. While he was going to the seboxon clinic he was doing good, but that didn't start until later.

In April, my brother that skipped the state back when he was seventeen and lived in Florida called me. We talked and he asked how long our mother had been gone. I told him "twenty seven years today". He said, "Today?" I said, "Yes, it's April eightteenth". He got quiet and was upset. He told me his eighteen year old daughter wasn't speaking to him. That's my little niece. She grew up. He lost his construction business and was being evicted. I told him that I just bought a house and it has an extra room and he can come home to Delaware and live with me. He asked me to do something for him and to call him the next night. The next night when I called he was hanging from a tree. I flew his body back home and buried him in one of my plots next to my father. My sister and I flew our niece up from down south where she and my brother were living. For the funeral Sue either flew in from Florida, her dad's or was living there. She was in and out so much I couldn't keep track. I believe she came from somewhere because she had her clothes in a suitcase that Anthony rummaged through. While Sue was there Anthony got into her belongings and stole a hundred and twenty dollars and then had the nerve to tell her that he took it to go get drugs. Sue came to me crying and I gave her a hundred and twenty dollars of my own money. I also flew into Anthony. I made him go into a rehab and Sue and her cousin took him there and made sure he was signed in as a patient. He was only there a week or so then he was being released. I knew this wasn't good. He needed extensive treatment. Six months to a year was what I was thinking, not a week. A week is detox. I remember once he was on house arrest at our new home because I had to make sure he didn't go anywhere. He was wearing a monitor anklet. When he was on probation no one could be on the phone after ten o'clock at night because that was when the house arrest officer started checking to make sure he was in the house. He could call from ten to twelve midnight. They dropped by whenever they felt like it. Anthony was never put back into jail for violating probation. It was always new trouble that landed him in jail. When we had the guy renting the room and Anthony had to go to jail for something he had done he was put in a work release program. Anthony's job was to work in the kitchen and help prepare breakfast for the other inmates. The inmates would stay awake until three or four o'clock in the morning talking and making noise. Anthony had to get up at five to start working in the kitchen and he was always tired because he never got any sleep. One Friday night he called me and asked me to come get him. I asked if they let him go. He replied, "No, I left". I yelled at him and told him to hurry and go back. He said he couldn't because he jumped over the wall. I went to where he was and picked him up and brought him home. No sense in taking him right back. The damage was already done. Saturday I talked him into turning himself into the police on Sunday. Sunday night at eight o'clock I took him to the police station and sat in the car and watched as he walked into the building and told them what he had done. This was another charge on him. Felony escape after conviction. He was not on any bi-polar medication and we didn't know we had the disease, yet. Otherwise, I'm sure he might have thought first instead of acting on impulse as you do when you are bi-polar.

At the small wake my homeless brother saw my house for the first time and exclaimed, "Wow, no wonder you didn't want me to know where you lived". He has slept on one of my sofas several times since then. Other than being on my sofa occasionally he has lived out of his truck for the last five years. I paid him to fix two of my ceilings. The front porch and the back family room had ceilings that you could look right at the stars through. The previous owner did not have the money to put a new roof on the house. She was fifty two years old and one night after she got off of work her sister found her dead from an aneurysm on the front porch. We had to rip down the wet soggy ceiling tiles and put up dry sheet rock after we repaired where the roof was leaking. Then my brother sanded and painted the ceiling with popcorn paint. He did the same with the back room family room addition. I paid him and he went right out and bought beer and came back and proceeded to get drunk. Of course we had words. He was not going to treat me like he did at his house in my own home. He left and stayed away for a while and then when the weather got real cold he came back and I let him on the sofa. He had slept in his truck so many winters that he burned the heating coil and didn't have the money to fix it. Last September he was staying with me and he went out and I didn't see him until three o'clock in the morning. He was drunk and yelling in my bedroom window to let him in. I wouldn't and now he is staying with a friend. Sue said he is starting to get SSI for his depression and bi-polar and he is living with a friend and going to pay him rent. He owes me two hundred dollars for paying his truck insurance so his tags weren't pulled by motor vehicle. I don't expect him to return it, although I could use it.

I planted a huge garden the first summer in my new home. I planted two dwarf apple trees, 2 seedless (that have seeds) grape vines, 2 blueberry bushes, 20 strawberry plants, all kinds of spices, tomato plants, squash, cucumbers, lima beans and flowers. I love gardening. It is therapeutic for me but it kills my back. I was out of work again and on bereavement leave. I didn't care if I ever went back to work. I loved staying home, but I had to work to have a home. That first year Joey and my granddaughter were always at my house. It was wonderful. They were just six houses away, but Joey wanted to move to a bigger house with a garage. I cried every time he mentioned moving. I didn't want to hold him back and finally I accepted the fact that he was eventually going to move. I went into a deep depression that lasted months. When I started to come out of it something else would happen. This time I was to give Anthony a ride to probation. I had rented a room out to a sloppy guy and was putting him out. I called the house to see if Anthony was ready to go to probation. The renter answered and said Anthony was in his room and he was going to let him use his car to go. I kept working and something kept knawing at my stomach. Finally half an hour later I went home for lunch. I went straight to Anthony's room. He was lying on the floor incoherent and gurgling. A note was on the bed. It said "Forgive me mom. I'm sorry. I can't get off the drugs. I love you, Anthony." As I write this there are certain things that start me crying and I can't stop. This was one of them. I called 911 and they came to the house and put the paddles on him in his room. Did he stop breathing on me? They took him in the ambulance and I followed. The hospital staff kept him in an induced coma for two or three days. When he awoke he stayed in the hospital for five days then came home. They wrote it up as an overdose. I never showed anyone the note he left. I took FMLA to stay home and watch him. I have been through so much with him. He's part of me. I would rather die than have anything happen to any of my children or grandchildren. Staying home was a happy time for me even with all the drama happening. Finally I went back to work. Not because I wanted to but because the Dr. made me. He wouldn't keep me out any longer to watch Anthony. Back to work I went and this day it was time for Anthony to go to probation again. I called the house and the renter said that he let

Anthony borrow his car and he already left and wasn't back, yet. I thought nothing of it. When I came home from work Anthony still was not there. The renter called the police around eight o'clock that night and reported his car stolen. Anthony called me at three o'clock in the morning to come into the city to get him. I asked where the car was and he said he didn't have it. I went into the city and while I was looking for the place my son was I saw a big African American driving the renter's car. I followed him and pulled up next to him. I said "Do you know that car has been reported stolen? He took off fast . The next morning one of Anthony's drug friends called him and told him where he could pick the car up at. Anthony had to go to court for this charge even though he was given the keys and permission to borrow the car. There were some other misdemeanors tacked on. He ended up doing 30 days in jail and in the meantime I got the renter out of my house. Sue had told me that the renter was selling drugs out of my house on his computer and going to USPS to mail the drugs to the people. I was in shock. These were drugs that were prescribed to him for his mental status and here he was selling them. He didn't give me any trouble about getting out because I threatened to call the police. I don't think I'll rent anymore.

Sue, Anthony and I are living together again like we should be. Then Anthony and Sue got into another argument and she packed up and moved to her father's house. It was around Thanksgiving and I cooked the traditional dinner for Anthony and me. The next day Anthony and I got into an argument while I was on the phone with Joey. Anthony was playing with one of his knives that he collects and arguing with me. Joey heard him and called the police when we hung up. Anthony and I stopped arguing and I made two turkey sandwiches for us and we were watching a movie and eating leftovers when our Belgian Shepherd, who was lying on the floor in front of us, looked at the front door and barked. I got up to see what she was barking at and saw about a dozen police officers all pointing guns at me and yelling to open the door. I'm telling you, somebody has to do something about these Police Department. I yelled at them "No, get off my property". They kept yelling back and finally came into my front porch and were getting ready to kick the door to the house in when Anthony opened it. They attacked us. What else is new? They took Anthony and arrested him for something and left me home. Not being on any medication, or even knowing I needed medication, I went to the garage and turned my car on and pretended I was cleaning the car when actually I was going to commit suicide by H

O. I passed out on the back seat with the music blaring (stupid) and the next door neighbors called the police. They came and yanked me out of there and took me to the hospital. I swore up and down that I was cleaning the car and not trying to kill myself. The hospital left me sitting on a gurney unattended and I got up, took off their little alarm they attached to me and walked out the door right in time to see Joey pulling up. I jumped into his truck and yelled "Come on! Get me out of here!" He took me home and told me to go in and go straight to bed so the cops wouldn't know I was there, but right after he dropped me off at my house, before I reached the front door, here comes a policeman. I was caught. Back to the hospital I went. This time the hospital kept me until three in the morning and then said I could go but I should wait for daylight. Wait nothing. I started walking home. I knew Joey had to get up at five o'clock to go to work so I didn't want to bother him, so I just walked. I got home at five thirty in the morning. The hospital was around ten miles away, maybe a little less, but it took me from three until five thirty to get home. It was cold and I only had socks on. I can't remember when Anthony was released. He came home maybe later that day. I know he was home for Christmas because around New Year's Eve we had another run in with the police over Anthony and me arguing. This time they had the whole swat team out front of all the neighbors' houses aiming guns at my house, while yelling for Anthony to come out. He went out onto the front step and I immediately jumped in front of him. He kept telling me to move and I kept telling him, "No, can't you see they want to shoot you?" I screamed at the police "Shoot me if you want to shoot someone! Come on, sissies! Shoot me and leave my child alone. He hasn't done anything for you to be acting like this". Finally Anthony walked from behind me and started walking to the police, while I had the video camera aimed at the entire scene. If they were going to shoot my child I was going to have proof of what really happened. They took him away and I was so upset over everything that had happened I sliced both my wrists. The Drs said I almost decapitated one hand. After I sliced my wrists I laid down on the sofa to bleed out. I awoke, freezing, around six or seven in the morning. The darned dogs had licked my blood flow and stopped it and caused it to clot. Darn, if I had of known this would happen I would have locked them in another room. I was soaking wet with blood and freezing. I stood up to go to my room and change into warm pajamas and I fell flat on my face. My nose started bleeding. I tried a couple more times but I could not stand, probably from loss of so much blood. I finally crawled to my room using my elbows since my hands were cut and hurting. I managed to change and climb into bed and cover up to go to sleep. I fell asleep and the phone rang. It is Anthony and he wants me to come pick him up. I tell him I can't and finally after a while I tell him why I can't. He hung up and called the ambulance. I tried to go back to sleep but the phone kept ringing. Now it was the police. I told them "I'm fine, leave me alone". "You've done enough to me and Anthony". They were relentless and finally I allowed them to take me to the hospital. I spent New Year's Eve in the hospital and three more days. Then they transferred me to a psychiatric facility and I was stuck in there for two weeks before Anthony and Sue got me out of there. They got me out of there on January eighteenth twenty twelve, and we went straight to the funeral of their older half-sister who had eaten a gun. The girl was born to another woman a year before Anthony was born. Their dads were the same but Alex never acknowledged the girl as his child. It was impossible not to. She could have been Sue's twin! After my children got me out of the hospital I went on FMLA, again. I was out of work and living it up until the Drs said I could go back to work on February twentieth. I hated that job and working outside of the home. I had been living in my new home now for two years and the police had been there more than me. Sue remained living at her father's house, all the while writing a book about her imagined horrible childhood and Anthony and I. We didn't know it though. She was still being civil and associating with us, while slandering and defaming us all the while. Anthony and I ended up getting no contact orders on her. I will never forget the things she wrote about us. I contacted a lawyer and had the book taken out of print.

The day before my no contact order was up on her she mailed me a letter asking forgiveness and saying she wasn't on medication and would I please talk to her again. It just so happened that it was her birthday and I was on the phone with Anthony from the jail. I called Sue and we had a three way conversation. She was so happy, she cried. I told her Happy Birthday and she was happy to hear me on the phone. Of course I will forgive her. I am a Christian and it is the Christian thing to do, not to mention she is my daughter. Things were bad though for a while. I took her out of my will and disowned her, but I've since put her back. Life continued on. I bought two new doors for my house that I am constantly fixing up. With Sue and Anthony separated my stress level has gone down considerably and I can almost function. My mind will not let me forget the book that Sue wrote that drove me to try to commit suicide once more.

Everything is going well except for some arguments between Anthony and Sue. A couple were violent. Anthony has been in every rehab in the state of Delaware and Southern Pennsylvania. I was working twelve hour days reviewing food stamp and Medicaid cases at my job for a health and social services facility. I have a very bad back and had to work in pain. When I got off of work that particular night I walked in the door and the first thing I saw was two sinks in the kitchen piled sky high with dirty dishes. I have two adult children home all day and I screamed. We ended up in a big argument again and I told them both to leave after Anthony threw kerosene on me. I didn't want Sue to leave but she lied to the police to make me look like I was wrong. They went to their father's. Anthony only lasted a few months there and then his father threw him out in January. Anthony called me and I told him to come home. Sue stayed all the while writing a defamatory book about Anthony and me. Her step mother paid to have it published and it was so bad I sought out an attorney. I had the book taken out of print and the file destroyed. I called the publisher and told her that things in the book were not true and she used our real names. The publisher told me that my daughter submitted signed releases from everyone and I had to tell the publisher that I never signed one and Sue's brother never signed one. The publisher contacted Sue and told her she was tearing up her file and not going to print anymore books because she had lied. This infuriated Sue so much that she called my labor relations at my job and told them that I closed her food stamp and Medicaid case. The labor relations girl told Sue that I did not have the capability to do that. She would have to call her worker. Sue then asked the girl how the state could hire someone with such an extensive criminal background. She was told that the state does not do background checks on everyone. Also, I did not have anything serious to keep me from being hired. After all, this was the third time they hired me! Next she called my pain management Dr,(for my bad back) and told him I was not taking my medication, I was selling it. After going to this Dr for seven years he believed one telephone call. Now I missed even more work. I could sit at my desk no more than an hour before my back was on fire and no Dr would help me because of what my daughter said. I worked in agony for a year than things turned around. I found another pain management that after I explained the entire story to them, they accepted me. Sue and her step mother also called the state police and told them that on a Saturday in September I was riding back and forth in front of their house yelling things out of the window. When I got to work Monday morning I received a telephone call from a state trooper and I told him about Sue being on the brink of being psychotic that I did not do that. First, they lived an hour and a half away from me. I drive a gas guzzling SUV and I'm not going to waste my gas on them. Second, it was Separation Day in olde New Castle. The day Delaware broke away from the thirteen colonies and New Castle celebrates it every year on a Saturday in September and it just so happened that I was there all day and had two witnesses to the fact. The officer said he thought something seemed odd about those two, meaning Sue and her step mother. Bi-polar people who are not on medication do impulsive things and never give up once they set their mind to do something. I was a nervous wreck not knowing what my daughter was going to do next. I read the first half of her book and cried the entire time. I didn't read any further.

{12}

From June until September I cried all the time. I couldn't work. Anthony and I took her to family court and got no contact orders on her so she would be arrested if she bothered us again. Finally I went to a shrink in September and got on a mood stabilizer, antidepressants and anxiety medication. I still cry when I think of what my daughter said about me in that book. She is my only daughter. I love her more than life and I never had any idea she felt the way she did about me. I had a break down and had to go on FMLA, again. This is also when I found out I am Bi-polar /major manic depressive. Everything was interfering with my work. I was having black out spells, wobbling and nearly fainting for a year. Everyone commented about it. Even the people at work thought I was drinking. This was before I went out of work on FMLA. I kept telling the Dr. every time I went to her and she just shrugged it off. Then one day I went to the grocery store to get a prescription and saw a co-worker there. I was out on sick leave again at the time. We walked out of the store together and I was standing next to her car window talking to her when I felt that fainting feeling coming upon me. I told my co-worker that I felt faint and I had to sit for a minute or two. She said that she watched me in her side mirror, I was parked behind her, and first my head started shaking violently and then my knees started shaking and then I started to go down. The next thing I remember is her holding me up and calling my

name. The co-worker drove me home and later my daughter-in-law
drove me to get my car. Joey lived six houses down the street from
where I bought my house in twenty ten. I bought it to be near him and
my grandchildren. When we went to get my car I went into the drug
store and asked the pharmacist what drug was I on that would cause
me to have seizures. He said "You are on a seizure medication". I said,
"I know, but I don't have seizures". He said it was Lamictal. The mood
stabilizer that the shrink had me on and I had been telling her for a
year about the black outs. I immediately stopped taking the Lamictal
and haven't had a spell since. It's been ten months since then. I'm
also looking for a new Dr.Anthony started going to the community
college in 2012. He was taking two majors. He was taking Human
Services and Drug and Alcohol counselor. He was getting up at five
thirty every morning and driving six miles to get medication called
Seboxon to keep him from wanting to do drugs. It was a cash only
deal and Anthony paid them four hundred dollars a month out of
his seven hundred and twenty one dollar SSI check. I must admit he
was doing well. He would then come home and go to school. He was
always at his computer doing his homework. One semester he had a
4.0 average and received a certificate from the Dean of the college.
For two and a half years Anthony did this, and then it came time for
him to actually do an internship. During my old Social Worker days
I worked with a fellow who was now the supervisor at my old service
center. I e-mailed him and he contacted an administrator and they
arranged for Anthony to do his two hundred hours at the service
center. They made him his own office. He determined eligibility
for a social health care program and he really enjoyed helping the
people that came for help. Anthony is a people person and he will
give you the shirt off his back. Some days when he wasn't at the
service center he was at school taking classes morning and night. I
told him he had too much on his plate. Around Christmas he had
some trouble with a girl he was dating. He is very sensitive and I don't
know if it was the trouble with the girl or if he had too much on his
plate but unbeknownst to me he stopped taking the seboxon and
started using cocaine and crack cocaine again. He was still going
to school and to the service center. Everyone at the service center
and the administrator had high opinions and praise for him. The
administrator was even helping him get a permanent job with the
state as a social worker, following in his mother's footsteps. Spring
semester started on May second and that was also the last day of the
internship. The report from the supervisor and administrator had

nothing but good things to say about Anthony. May second, even though my job was on shaky ground, Anthony and I went to the car dealership and I bought a twenty eleven Acura with a six hundred and forty a month payment. I wasn't on my bi-polar medication anymore and here I am making unreasonable and impulsive purchases. Anthony did not come home on Saturday night. I called him and his cell phone went straight to voice mail. I was really worried. I called all morning on Sunday and he wouldn't answer. Finally around noon he called me because I saw his name and number come up on the television, however, the phone did not ring. I answered it and it hung up. This happened three times in a row before I realized the phone was probably off the hook in Anthony's room. I went into his mess of a room and finally found the phone and put it back on the hook. I then went back to my seat and waited for him to call again. I should have called him and I don't know why I didn't. He called three times in a row, why didn't I suspect something? I should have called him immediately but I didn't and I don't know why not. He never called back until around two o'clock. When I answered he told me he was arrested and in jail. I died, again. I asked him "why". And he said "for the same thing". I said, "What same thing?" He kept saying, "You know". No, I didn't know. He got into so much trouble I didn't know what he did. Finally he said the "Wawa" and I said robbery? And he said yes. My world ended right then. Here comes another breakdown. I have them a lot. I definitely am not as strong as people keep telling me I am. He said his bail was forty thousand dollars cash. I fell apart. I cried and cried and went to work the next day, Monday, but I left after half a day. I could not concentrate on my work and all I did was cry. I had an office with a door by myself. Every single case that I checked over and handed into the supervisor she found something wrong with it and waited until she had about twenty cases and then brought them all back to me at once to correct. Most of the time the paperwork was in the case and she didn't see it. I felt like she was out to get rid of me because I was sixty one. I had watched her make things so difficult for three other people over sixty that they retired. One man, a clerk, came to work while he was having a stroke. A co-worker told him to go to the hospital but he said he was fine. That weekend he had a massive stroke and is now in a nursing home/physical therapy place in Philadelphia where his sister lives. He's been there over a year and he will not be back. All the new hires are in their twenties and thirties. I contacted a lawyer and he said I definitely have a case but with everything else going on in my life I just don't think I want to be bothered. I had my shrink keep me out of work indefinitely. I went on the state's short term disability. I turned sixty two on July eighteenth and I immediately told human resources that I planned to retire effective October first.

I collected short term disability from my job until October and in October I got my first retirement check and a small pension check came on the last day of the month. Working for the state of Delaware has been the worse job I have ever had in my 62 years and I have been working since I was 15. And as far as that supervisor goes, this is one time I hope, what goes around, comes around. When I went out sick in June I immediately applied for social security disability and it was approved and started in December. I am now officially retired and on disability. I had over six thousand dollars in a savings at my job and when I retired I was able to with draw it. I did not bail Anthony out of jail. He has been there for ten months and will be sentenced on March twenty seventh, next Friday. I used the money to hire him a darn good attorney rather than pay bail. I have had my crying and dark cloud days more since he got arrested. He was doing so well. I don't know what happened. He's an Agent Orange baby, as is Sue, and I'm sure that has something to do with their diagnosis and problems. Anthony was on the right path for over three years so I know he can do it. I have been out of work now for ten months and this was a job that I had always received "distinguished" on my performance reviews.

While in Florida when I was taking the Humanities class it actually turned out to be an art class. I had to go to the local art museum and interpret the paintings that were in there. I also had to paint four pictures to pass the class. I painted Jesus on the cross, a woman drying herself off after bathing, myself, and the Virgin Mary. The Virgin Mary was so good that the professor kept it and was showing it to the other classes how things were done. I passed that class with an "A".

To fill my days I have started painting again while fighting to help my son get out of jail. I have not tried to hurt myself since getting on Bi-polar medication over two years ago. I am not really good at painting, but it is a hobby and I am told I'm good by people. I guess I am better than some. A girl wanted to buy a picture of an eight by ten angel that I did for sixteen dollars and fifty cents. I didn't sell it. I will give it to Sue, maybe. Monday I will go to a new Dr. to see if I can get new and better Bi-polar/Major Manic Depressive medication. What I am taking helps, but I still am depressed.

Around October and November I started going to the Senior Center and painting ceramics. I painted a pearl white Christmas tree for Sue. It has her name on it's base and it has lights to plug in and light up. I painted myself one, too. Years ago when Anthony and Sue were small we would paint ceramics. At the time there was a ceramic shop close by so that we could buy our materials and pieces to paint. I believe Anthony painted a ghost and Sue did a pumpkin. The store is no longer there or I would still be doing ceramics. The senior center lady takes too long and I do not have the patience to wait for her to take us to the next step. When I do something I like to do it and get it done. It is just Anthony's Rottweiler, Cleopatra, and me, now. When he calls I put the speaker phone on so Cleo can hear him. I know she misses him. He would walk her every day and she slept in his bed with him. Now she only gets walked in the warm months and she sleeps on the floor next to my bed. I would love to breed her, but it seems everyone is against breeding these days. Maybe someday we'll meet a nice looking male Rotti. I miss when my children were small, before they went to school and learned things that weren't taught at home by other children and before the stealing, lying and violent fights started.

October third Joey moved. He bought a four bedroom house with a two car garage on an acre and a half of land in a better area a half an hour away from me. He is in his element. His property backs up to farmland and deer and foxes are always in his yard. I spent their first Thanksgiving with them and was invited for Christmas, but I stayed home. On nice days I will take a ride to their house to visit my grandchildren. My eight year old granddaughter is usually in school, but my two year old grandson is at home. He is adorable. He is also an August baby like Anthony. My son says I am the only one that he does not drive crazy. He and I can get on the same level; where his parents can't. Cancers are eternal children and one bad habit is getting too involved with children on their own level. It helps for understanding them when no one else can, though. Joey got a rototiller and we are making plans to plant a big vegetable garden on his land this summer. It will also teach my grandchildren good skills, also. I miss having them six houses down the street. Sometimes I will forget they are not there and look down the street to see if Joey is home from work, yet. I had thought of renting a room out to have some companionship, but after the last fiasco with a renter I decided not to. After Anthony went to jail last May, Joey would come up every week and cut my grass. He stopped after work a couple of times and shoveled snow for me, too. He works five minutes away. My back will not let me cut grass or shovel snow My brain tumor, five tumors on my liver and a small cyst on the tail of my pancreas along with the bipolar still make me disabled. I keep in touch with a couple of people at my job who were true friends, otherwise I do not miss working at all. I am quite happy to be at home all day and do what I want when I want. On a warm day I will get a friend and we will meet at a Park and walk the three mile walk to keep from getting fat. She is my age but she has been retired for ten years because she put thirty years in with the state. Sue and I talk on the phone every day and she is coming for a visit on the twenty seventh. She is doing very well and I am happy for her and very proud of her. We have come a long way in our relationship as compared to two years ago. Also, the three of us now know that we are Bi=polar/Manic Depressive and on medication for it. Life looks a whole lot better now that we are taking medication. No matter how many times I tried to throw the towel in and failed, I am now glad that I did fail, because this is the beginning of a new chapter in my life. A good chapter and a good life are just the beginning.